EXAM CRAM™

Certification Success

MCSE • MCSD
CNE • CNA
A+ • CISCO
ORACLE • SUN/JAVA

Ed Tittel

Certification Success Exam Cram

Limits of Liability and Disclaimer of Warranty

Trademarks

The Coriolis Group, LLC
14455 N. Hayden Road, Suite 220
Scottsdale, Arizona 85260

602/483-0192
FAX 602/483-0193
http://www.coriolis.com

Library of Congress Cataloging-in-Publication Data
Tittel, Ed.
Certification success exam cram / by Ed Tittel
p. cm.
Includes index.
ISBN 1-57610-422-2
1. Electronic data processing personnel--Certification--Computer programs. I. Title.
QA76.3.T5734 1999
004--dc21 98-45720
CIP

Printed in the United States of America
10 9 8 7 6 5 4

Publisher
Keith Weiskamp

Acquisitions Editor
Shari Jo Hehr

Marketing Specialist
Cynthia Caldwell

Project Editor
Jeff Kellum

Production Coordinator
Meg E. Turecek

Cover Design
Anthony Stock

Layout Design
April Nielsen

CD-ROM Developer
Robert Clarfield

CORIOLIS

Our readers tell us why

Certification Insider Press *is* #1

Thank you for writing and making available the valuable *Exam Cram* series of books. I not only passed the NT Server 4 in the Enterprise exam but also scored very high. I give credit to the very readable and understandable *Exam Cram* books. It is not only the subjects you cover but also the exam-taking tips and strategies which pull one through the rough parts of the exam.

– Richard Peppel

The *Exam Crams* are by far the best studying companions! Since discovering your study guides, I have been able to cut my study time in half. They are indispensable for those who are engaged in self-study programs. Thank you!

—Michael Dominguez, MCSE

I owe a great deal to the *Exam Cram* series. The specifics given in the books relate to exactly what you need to know for the exam. I made sure the Cram Sheet was the last thing I read before taking the tests. They are compiled with very important information that leads to success in test taking and passing.

—David M. Peak, MCP

I want to say a huge thank you. I used your books for Workstation, Server, Enterprise, and Networking Essentials. I can honestly say I would not have achieved certification as quickly as I did without using your books.

—Clayton Doige, MCSE

I have used the *Exam Cram* series for three of the six exams I have taken. I achieved over 90% on all three! The books are affordable, readable, and understandable and get to the point quickly, making it easier to learn the material for the exam with minimum outlay and effort. Well done.

—Douglas Bell

See for yourself why we're #1 and drop us a line at **craminfo@coriolis.com**— *we look forward to hearing about your testing-successes!*

CORIOLIS

14455 North Hayden, Suite 220 • Scottsdale, Arizona 85260

The Smart Way To Get Certified SM

Thank you for purchasing *Certification Success Exam Cram*, the one book that brings together information on the numerous certifications available today.

Certification Insider Press was created in late 1997 by The Coriolis Group to help professionals obtain certification and advance their careers. Achieving certification involves a major commitment and a great deal of hard work. To help you reach your goals, we've listened to our readers, and have designed our entire product line around the way they like to study, learn, and master challenging subjects. Our approach is *The Smart Way to Get Certified.*

In less than a year, Coriolis has published over one million copies of our highly popular *Exam Cram*, *Exam Prep*, and *On Site* guides. Our *Exam Cram* books, specifically written to help you pass an exam, are the number one certification self-study guides in the industry. They are the perfect complement to any study plan you have, as well as to the rest of the *Certification Insider Press* series: *Exam Prep*, comprehensive study guides designed to help you thoroughly learn and master certification topics, and *On Site*, guides that really show you how to apply your skills and knowledge on the job.

Our commitment to you is to ensure that all of the certification study guides we develop help you save time and frustration. Each one provides unique study tips and techniques, memory joggers, custom quizzes, insight about test taking, practical problems to solve, real-world examples, and much more.

Good luck with your certification and your career. Thank you for allowing us to help you achieve your goals.

Keith Weiskamp

Keith Weiskamp
Publisher, Certification Insider Press

About The Author

Ed Tittel is the Series Editor for the *Certification Insider Press Exam Cram* series, and has personally contributed to over half of the titles currently available in that series. A contributor to over 70 computer-related books, Tittel has written on topics as diverse as *Stupid PC Tricks* (Addison-Wesley, 1991) to study guides on Windows NT Workstation 4 and Networking Essentials.

Ed is also a member of the Program Committee and the faculty for the NetWorld + Interop trade show, where he specializes in network operating systems and Internet technologies. In a past life, Ed worked for Novell, Inc., where his last job was Director of Technical Marketing. In that capacity, he oversaw technical content for trade shows and the BrainShare developer's conference, prior to his departure in 1994. Since then, Ed has presided over LANWrights, Inc., a small writing and consulting company, where he spends his time writing, teaching, and researching networking topics.

In his spare time, Ed is a devoted, if indifferent, pool player, and likes to cook (especially homemade stock, and all the good things that come from it). Ed and his trusty Labrador retriever, Blackie, make their home in Austin, Texas. You can reach Ed via email at **etittel@lanw.com**, or through his Web site at **www.lanw.com**.

Acknowledgments

To Kurt Hudson, for planting the seed that sprouted *Exam Cram*, thanks a million! Your offhand remarks and initial steps down this path gave me the inspiration to create this series.

To Dawn Rader, James Michael Stewart, and Mary Burmeister, who helped me prune and trim the results, thanks even more. Without you, and the rest of the LANWrights crew, we could never have achieved the many milestones along the road to success.

To Keith Weiskamp, Shari Jo Hehr, and the rest of the crew at Coriolis, who made *Exam Cram* turn into a raging monster, thanks for believing in me, and for giving me a voice in the way all this turned out. I appreciate your efforts, your insights, but most of all, your passion and enthusiasm.

To my parents, Ceil and Al Tittel, thanks for being there for me when I needed it, and for helping me lay the foundation that created a love of language and technology, and the courage to go it alone.

To my sister, Kathy, not to mention Mike, Helen, and Colin: You guys are too much! I'm glad I know you, and that you can give me regular doses of reality, Virginia-style.

To my friends, especially Yvonne, Tressa, Robert, and others too numerous to mention: Thanks for listening to me rant about work when that's what I needed to do, and even more for distracting me when that's what I needed even more. You guys have helped me keep my life together.

To my readers: Thanks for your feedback, both good and bad, but thanks even more for voting for our work and ideas with your hard-earned money. I can only hope that you continue to find value in what we do from here on out!

Ed Tittel
Austin, Texas
September 12, 1998

Table Of Contents

Introduction

Welcome to *Certification Success Exam Cram*! This book is aimed squarely at people who are curious about the computer certifications that are popping up in today's marketplace. If you're intrigued by the occasional bits of alphabet soup you see in the magazines or in the classified ads for "Engineering/Technical" jobs, you've come to the right place.

By the time you finish this book, you'll know the difference between an MCSE and a CCIE. In fact, you should even be able to understand what it takes to start stringing some of these initials behind your own name—especially how much work and expense are involved and what steps you need to take along the way.

In short, this book is intended to explain some of the most popular, if not most important, computer certifications available. As you read this book, you should also get a good idea about what's involved in obtaining such certifications, and how well these certifications might match your computing interests.

The Certification Game

Although the details vary widely from program to program, all certification programs have certain elements in common. These common elements are discussed in Chapter 1. The rest of this book takes these common elements and explains how certification programs sponsored by the six leading organizations fit this model.

Most of the certification programs covered in this book, in keeping with the current state of the computing industry, are vendor-sponsored programs. In other words, companies such as Microsoft, Novell, Oracle, Cisco, and Sun Microsystems create complex products or technologies. To make sure that they can sell these products or technologies to their customers, among other things, they must be able to guarantee a supply of knowledgeable, competent individuals who can use these products to get things done. In the simplest of terms, this explains why certification is important to vendors in particular—it's an important part of the overall delivery system that's necessary to introduce complex products and technologies to the marketplace.

Some certification programs—in particular Computing Technology Industry Association's (CompTIA's) A+ and its planned Network+ credentials—are created by groups of industry players for everyone's benefit. These types of certifications are usually called *vendor-neutral*, to indicate that they stress general knowledge as opposed to detailed knowledge of some particular vendor's proprietary products or technologies.

Given that certification is good for vendors and employers alike, you might ask, "What's in it for me?" Answering this question requires separating hype from reality. The vendors will tell you that their certifications are the keys to career success, if not liberty and the pursuit of happiness. Employers like certification credentials because they define measurable steps up job ladders, and because certifications make it easy for them to separate motivated, trained employees or job applicants from others.

But, the marketplace decides what a certification is really worth. If you don't see the initials for some certification program anywhere in the classifieds, or if you've never even heard of that program, that might mean it's not a very valuable credential. On the other hand, some of these seemingly innocuous strings of letters can be a ticket to a distinct improvement in your financial circumstances. However, certification is not cheap, easy, or free. This book should help you understand the details of the specific programs I cover, examine and evaluate other certification programs, and decide which ones are worthwhile—and which ones to ignore.

Interesting Certification Stats

Today, technical training and certification is becoming an industry niche of its own. Like other such niches, it has its share of focused publications, including magazines like *Inside Technology Training*, *Microsoft Certified Professional Magazine*, *The NetWare Connection*, and numerous others. Industry analysts—like the Gartner Group, IDC, and the Meta Group, among others—employ analysts to track this market niche, just as they track other niches to look for trends, seek out revenue opportunities, and advise companies whether or not they should jump onto the training and certification bandwagon.

Based on the reports from these various sources, the answer to "Is training and certification a worthwhile business activity?" appears to be a resounding "Yes!" Without trying to edit or analyze some of the reporting I uncovered when researching this topic, here are some interesting facts about certification programs that you might find surprising:

- The total population of computer-certified individuals in the United States today numbers less than 2 million. By the year 2000, that number is expected to jump to over 5 million; by the year 2010, to over 20 million. These are the kinds of numbers that not only attract interest, but spur serious investment.

- Many large companies—like Microsoft, Novell, Oracle, Cisco, and others—make serious money from their training and certification programs. For the larger companies, I'm talking hundreds of millions of dollars a year; for smaller companies, tens of millions of dollars annually. Not enough to dominate the bottom line, but more than enough to constitute a worthwhile investment.

- Reports about the value of certification—especially those from vendors (and if you poke around the vendor Web sites I mention, you can find plenty of these for yourself)—stress ROI, or "Return on Investment," for certified employees. In English, this means they're more productive, fix problems faster, and don't need to wait on hold as often for technical support because they can fix many problems themselves.

- For individuals, certification can mean an increase in salary, or a better job elsewhere. The vendor Web sites for certification programs invariably include profiles of certification overachievers, called "Success Stories." Although it's wise to take some of the claims (and dollar figures) with a grain of salt, there's no denying that certification can boost your bottom line, too. Most salary surveys show that certified technical staff earn at least 15 to 20 percent more than their uncertified counterparts. The only caveat I'd add to this observation is that certification may get you in the door, but it's what you know that will keep you on the job. Be sure to learn how to use what you know, or you won't be able to stay on the job very long. This means hands-on experience, which takes extra time and effort.

I could go on with these amazing and wonderful statistics for quite some time, but hopefully, you get the idea: Certification is a growing market, and is creating opportunities for both certifiers and certificants. The devil is in the details, though, and that's what this book is supposed to help you with. So please, read on!

About This Book

This book consists of seven chapters, followed by an afterword and glossary. Chapter 1 covers certification programs in a bit more detail, and gives an overview of the six specific organizations I cover in Chapters 2 through 7. Starting with Microsoft's various and sundry certifications, this book proceeds to explore Novell's programs, followed by Oracle's, then Cisco's, then CompTIA's, and concludes with a discussion of Sun's Java certification programs. The afterword mentions some certification programs that you might find interesting but are not covered in this book. It also provides a question and answer section to help you gauge which of the programs I do cover might best fit your technical interests and experiences. The glossary contains definitions of the terms you'll be introduced to throughout this book. Finally, the companion CD-ROM is a useful tool to use.

Each chapter in this book follows a regular structure and offers graphical cues about especially important or useful material. In fact, it's modeled on Certification Insider Press's popular *Exam Cram* series, which helps individuals prepare for most, if not all, of the certification exams mentioned in this book. Here's the structure—which I follow slavishly—of the chapters:

- **Opening hot lists** Each chapter begins with lists of the terms, tools, and techniques that you must learn and understand before you can be fully conversant with the chapter's subject matter. I follow the hot lists with one or two introductory paragraphs to set the stage for the rest of the chapter. Here, you'll find a brief description of the certification programs you're about to dive into, to help you get oriented.

- **Topical coverage** After the opening hot lists, each chapter covers the various certification programs and exams that are the focus of that chapter. This includes an overview of the programs, including the number of tests, their costs, how much time you're allotted to take them, and so on. Then it covers each program individually. This includes overviews of the topics that are likely to appear in the qualifying exams, and comments on the format and contents of these exams.

- **Visual elements** Within each chapter, I use visual elements to highlight particularly important or useful information about certification programs and exams. For instance, the Study Alert icon flags items of information that are particularly germane to the test-taking experience.

> STUDY ALERT
>
> This is what a Study Alert looks like. In a regular *Exam Cram*, a Study Alert stresses concepts, terms, software, or activities that will most likely appear in one or more certification test questions. In this book, however, they flag items that are particularly important to note or act upon relating to one or more certification tests.

On the other hand, the Tip icon flags useful or helpful information that may or may not be test-related, but that is certainly worth noting, because it can save you time, money, or effort.

TIP This is what a Tip looks like. In a regular *Exam Cram*, a Tip points out a shortcut, a time-saving technique, or some other fact that will save you time or effort. In this book, the Tip flags information that might help make your certification experience cheaper, faster, or easier.

Even if material isn't flagged as a Study Alert or a Tip, all the contents of this book are associated, at least tangentially, to something certification-related. This book is lean so that it can focus on explaining only the essential elements of these certification programs; you'll find that what appears in the meat of each chapter is critical knowledge.

- **Details and resources** Every chapter ends with a section titled "Need To Know More?". These sections provide direct pointers to the vendor's or organization's certification program data, as well as pointers to third-party resources that offer further details on the certification program or programs covered in a chapter. In addition, this section tries to rate the quality and thoroughness of the topic's coverage by each resource. If you find a resource you like in this collection, use it, but don't feel compelled to use all the resources. On the other hand, I recommend only resources I use on a regular basis, so none of my recommendations should waste your time or your money.

The Roadmap To Certification Success CD-ROM

This book's companion CD-ROM, titled "The Roadmap To Certification Success," is a useful tool for any would be certificant. Narrated by me, Ed Tittel, this interactive CD-ROM explains the intricate details of certification programs in general and highlights most of the programs discussed in this book. It also explains Certification Insider Press's concept of Learn It!, Pass It!, Do It! by introducing its three series—*Exam Prep*, *Exam Cram*, and *On Site*. It also has sample test questions to show you what you can expect when you finally take a certification test. Spend some time with this CD-ROM to familiarize yourself with the numerous certification programs and their intricacies.

How To Use This Book

If you're interested in certification in general, and don't have a specific area of technical expertise or experience, you might want to read this book from cover to cover. Some of the material that I present, to do proper justice to the certification programs I cover, gets pretty technical.

If you find yourself mystified by the terminology or concepts that I use to describe a certification program, chances are that you'll find the technical material necessary to obtain that certification downright opaque. For that reason, you should feel free to skip any material that doesn't make sense to you. If you really want to get to the bottom of anything, though, you can always visit the vendor's or organization's Web site to look for basic tutorials or to find information about introductory classes for a particular technology, product, or subject area. If you really want to learn any of this stuff, you can do it!

Given all the book's elements and its specialized focus, I've tried to create a tool to help you review the various certification programs I cover, and to perform meaningful comparisons between these programs (that's one reason why I've tried to make each chapter as consistent with the others as possible). I hope you can use it to help satisfy your curiosity about these programs, and to guide your progress into one or more of these certification areas.

But I know I can't please everyone, nor can I represent all this information completely or perfectly in such a short book. Therefore, please share your feedback on the book with me, especially if you have ideas about how I can improve it for future readers. I'll consider everything you say carefully, and I'll respond to all suggestions. You can reach me via email at **etittel@lanw.com**. Please remember to include the title of this book in your message; otherwise, I'll be forced to guess which book you're making a suggestion about. It's also a good idea to list a page number that relates to your questions or comments. I don't like to guess. I want to KNOW what you're thinking!

You should also visit Certification Insider Press's Web site at **www.certificationinsider.com**. I also maintain an *Exam Cram* Web site at **www.lanw.com/examcram/**.

Thanks, and enjoy the book!

1

Certification Programs

Terms you'll need to understand:

- √ Microsoft Certified Professional (MCP)
- √ Microsoft Certified Systems Engineer (MCSE)
- √ Microsoft Certified Solution Developer (MCSD)
- √ Microsoft Office User Specialist (MOUS)
- √ Certified Novell Administrator (CNA)
- √ Certified Novell Engineer (CNE)
- √ Master CNE (MCNE)
- √ Oracle Certified Professional (OCP)
- √ Cisco Career Certifications
- √ CompTIA A+
- √ Certified Java Programmer
- √ Certified Java Developer

Techniques you'll need to master:

- √ Identifying certification programs
- √ Locating certification training information online and offline
- √ Deciding which certification programs meet your needs, and those of your organization (or customer base)

Once you begin to pay attention to training and certification programs, you'll probably be amazed by the number of offerings available. You may even be a bit overwhelmed by the variety of programs to choose from, not to mention the many flavors of certification available. The key to success lies in selecting a certification credential that meets your career needs while also meeting the needs of current or prospective employers. In this chapter, you'll learn about the general characteristics of certification programs, and about some of the players, both large and small, who are involved in this game.

General Program Characteristics

Although the details of each individual certification program differ, all of them have a number of common elements. In fact, these programs usually include most, if not all, of the following characteristics:

- Identifies individuals who have demonstrated their knowledge and understanding of a particular technology or product.
- Defines a particular course of study, which may include supplementary materials. Such study materials can include classroom training, self-study materials, courseware, computer-based study materials, and trade books. Eventually, this course of study leads to a series of one or more tests that are aimed at examining an individual's knowledge of the subject matter. Most of these tests are computer-based and are widely available through nationwide (and global) testing centers.
- Certifies those who pass a prescribed test or set of tests for as long as the certification period lasts. When new products or technologies replace old ones, currently certified individuals must usually recertify to keep their certification current. Otherwise, such certifications lapse and become worthless.
- Offers tests in a monitored environment, for a fee, to would-be certificants. Each time an individual takes a certification test (whether he or she passes or fails), the test-taker must pay that fee. Some programs also limit the number of tries at a test within a given time period, but all such programs permit individuals to retake tests as many times as necessary to pass.
- Each vendor or organization maintains the individual's certification status that can be verified by current or potential employers.

Note: Some certifications are offered from software companies such as Novell and Microsoft, whereas others are offered from industry organizations such as the Computing Technology Industry Association (CompTIA). Therefore, I've differentiated between the two by using the word "vendor" when discussing certification programs offered from companies, and "organization" when discussing those offerings from vendor-neutral organizations.

Certified experts are available to help install, service, support, and maintain whatever technologies or products fall within the scope of their certification. This is important not only for vendors and industry organizations because of the impact it has on their customers, but also for those individuals who become certified. Access to a pool of certified experts adds to the credibility and usability of the products or technologies that these vendors and organizations support, and also adds to the technical competence of those who obtain certification. It's a win-win game, and a calculated way to maintain customer loyalty in all kinds of interesting ways, as you'll discover later in this chapter.

In addition to the common characteristics, there is another set of characteristics common to many certification programs:

- Certified individuals are granted the right to represent themselves as a "Certified ________," complete with camera-ready logo art for business cards, advertisements, and so on. As a result, such individuals can leverage the strength of their certification as a type of brand name.
- Certified individuals often are given special access to the vendor's or organization's technical support team. This includes discounts and information not made available to the general public.
- Certified individuals often qualify to receive evaluation copies of software products, participate in beta or early software release programs, and obtain access to password-protected Web sites, special mailing lists, and other sources of valuable "inside information."

TIP These perks add not just cachet to a certification, but also access to restricted or sensitive information, which can be of great value to individuals and the companies that employ them.

- Certified individuals who act as consultants may receive customer referrals from the certifying vendor or organization. In most cases, mailing lists and Web sites for certified individuals create well-informed groups of specialists.
- Certified individuals are often polled and surveyed to learn more about what they perceive and want, be it from products and services or from

the certification programs themselves. This provides the vendors with valuable information about their services and products from an educated user community. Also, certified individuals are often asked to participate in designing new elements for the certified curriculum, and to contribute questions to certification tests, which ultimately introduces new elements into a certification program.

The net result of certification programs is to create individuals who not only identify with the technologies or products around which their certification is based, but who also wear their credentials with a certain amount of pride. In most certification programs, there's a considerable sense of community, and of special status. After all, considerable time, expense, and effort are usually involved in obtaining a certification, and such certifications often increase the value of those who obtain them.

In fact, certification is generally regarded as a valuable program for vendors and organizations as an important credential for individuals to add to their resumes, and as an important checkbox for employers to add to their list of requirements for current and prospective employees. In the sections that follow, you'll learn more about what's at stake—and of value—for each of these separate constituencies, and why certification is an area where so many interests can converge so successfully.

Why Vendors Like Certification Programs

Although what you're about to read applies to organizations nearly as much as it does to vendors, certification programs can be particularly appealing to vendors beyond the value that access to a pool of certified experts can provide. In fact, a recent survey conducted by IDC indicated that 9 of the top 10 software vendors offer some type of certification program. Many of these vendors certify instructors to teach their curricula, and also offer some type of sales certification program, whereby resellers, distributors, and other elements of the sales channel can also demonstrate their knowledge and understanding of products, sales programs, and so on.

Certification can be a powerful weapon in any vendor's arsenal. Here's why:

- Vendors typically make money at all stages of a certification program: Many maintain their own training operations and charge authorized training centers to use their materials. They also offer official approvals for third-party training materials, study guides, and so on, and charge for the seal that usually accompanies such approval. They receive revenue from the testing centers that administer the tests. For large companies, such as Novell and Microsoft, training and certification is a business that generates hundreds of millions of dollars annually.

- Vendors maintain databases of all of their certified professionals, and therefore, automatically gain access to detailed demographic and employment information about the cream of the technical-professional crop. The value of these databases as sales and analysis tools is impossible to estimate.
- Those individuals who have shouldered the cost and effort involved in becoming certified are far more likely to want to maintain their certifications. This creates a captive audience of core business for future training and certification programs. Likewise, companies that fund employee certifications seek not only to maintain current certifications for those employees, but also often go to extraordinary lengths to retain them.

For vendors, certification adds up nicely: In addition to the money it generates, certification databases provide detailed information about key customers and guarantee the presence of "product champions" within those companies that employ certified professionals. I've observed three primary classes of vendors for whom certification is particularly useful or effective:

- Those who lead the market and wish to remain in that position
- Those who seek to capture a market and establish market dominance
- Those who seek to compete with market leaders on equal terms and are willing to bear the costs

Most vendors of any size in the high-tech marketplace fall into one of these categories, so the prevalence of certification programs should come as no surprise.

Why Individuals Like Certification Programs

In any profession, especially in high-tech organizations, good employees always seek to establish some type of professional advantage to elevate their status among their colleagues and peers. For technical employees, certifications have proven to be an effective tool in this effort. Certified employees tend to make more than their uncertified colleagues in similar job categories by anywhere from 10 to 25 percent.

But there's more to certification than just money. In a marketplace full of mergers and acquisitions, restructurings and layoffs can produce sudden employment shifts that require a special edge to merit consideration in both new and current positions. Many high-tech types have jumped on the certification bandwagon as a way to help them maintain ongoing employment, despite the constant change of employment at any one organization.. They definitely feel that certification makes it easier to find another job, no matter what circumstances may propel them into a job search.

Finally, for many motivated high-tech workers, there's a sense that obtaining a professional certification involves overcoming a challenge or obtaining a badge of accomplishment. Certainly, there are plenty of individuals who are certified across many programs, and some overachievers no sooner finish one such program than begin another.

Why Employers Like Certification Programs

Employers face the need for an increasingly diverse and complex array of skills in their employees, particularly in the areas of information technology (IT). Anything that can simplify their search for the right type of expertise—or that can help them bring existing employees up to the right level—is welcome.

That's why many companies require their employees in key positions—such as network administrator, system administrator, PC technician, or database administrator—to obtain and maintain certifications from the vendors and industry groups in which the organizations have made an investment. For some companies, the availability of training (if not certification) is a necessary precondition before they purchase a product or technology. "No certification, no sale" epitomizes the attitude in some boardrooms, in fact.

The Certification Programs

Now that you've explored the ingredients found in most certification programs, and the benefits for all the parties involved, it's time to introduce some of the key players in the certification game. In the sections that follow, you'll have a chance to read about some of the most profitable, best run, and most highly regarded certification programs in the IT business.

> Please note that not all technical professional certifications are covered in this book. For information about additional technical certifications, go to your favorite Internet search engine and search for keywords such as "certification," "training," and "exam." In addition, the best source of information on any certification is generally the vendor or organization that sponsors it, so always check with it first. Finally, I provide brief descriptions and pointers to additional certifications in this book's Afterword in the section titled "Other Certifications."

Microsoft Certification Programs

Microsoft's certification programs encompass neither the largest number of certificants nor the broadest range of offerings. However, as the "800-pound gorilla" of the software marketplace, Microsoft's programs are certainly generating the greatest amount of interest and activity. As you'd expect from a company like Microsoft, it offers a dizzying array of certifications whose requirements range from completing a single test to passing as many as nine tests.

Today, Microsoft claims over 300,000 certified professionals across its many designations, a population that is only surpassed by Novell's in size.

> At Microsoft's TechEd meeting in New Orleans in 1998, the company announced its intention to certify over one million professionals before the end of 1999. Given that its certifications now include certification in Microsoft Office products, and the size of the user base for Office alone, this goal does not seem excessively ambitious.

You will learn more about the details of Microsoft's certification programs in Chapter 2, but here's an overview of the seven different flavors of certification programs that are in store for you from the Microsoft camp:

- **Microsoft Office User Specialist (MOUS)** This program is at the bottom of the hierarchy. It certifies individuals who are proficient with Word, Excel, PowerPoint, and Access, usually for workers in an office environment. It is possible to certify as an expert in any one of these applications, and an additional "expert exam" on integrating multiple Office applications is also available.
- **Microsoft Certified Professional (MCP)** Passing almost any of the over 60 exams available in this program (except Networking Essentials, exam 70-058) qualifies an individual as an MCP. MCP status is a stepping stone to the much-vaunted Microsoft Certified Systems Engineer (MCSE) credential, which requires passing six tests.
- **MCP + Site Building (MCP+SB)** This program aims to certify individuals who can design, build, and maintain corporate Web sites. It requires that an individual first become an MCP, then pass any two from a pool of the three following tests:
  - **Designing and Implementing Web Sites with Microsoft FrontPage 98 (exam 70-055)** Covers Microsoft's Web site construction and maintenance toolkit.
  - **Designing and Implementing Commerce Solutions with Microsoft Site Server 3.0, Commerce Edition (exam 70-057)** Covers Microsoft's comprehensive electronic commerce Web site toolkit.

- **Designing and Implementing Web Solutions with Microsoft Visual InterDev 6.0 (exam 70-152)** Covers Microsoft's comprehensive Web-based application development toolkit.

- **MCP + Internet (MCP+I)** This program aims to certify individuals who can build and maintain an Internet presence using Microsoft Windows NT and related products. It requires passing three out of the four following tests:

  - **Internetworking with Microsoft TCP/IP on Microsoft Windows NT 4.0 (exam 70-059)** Covers basic IP networking and subnets, plus the protocols and services necessary to run an Internet site.

  - **Implementing and Supporting Microsoft Windows NT Server 4.0 (exam 70-067)** Covers basic proficiency in installing, configuring, and managing Windows NT Server 4.

  - **One of two exams on Microsoft Internet Information Server (IIS)** Covers IIS, Microsoft's Web server software; aimed at either the version 3 or 4 releases of IIS.

- **Microsoft Certified Systems Engineer (MCSE)** This program aims to certify systems engineers who can support networks built around (or that incorporate) Microsoft products, most notably, Windows NT. This program requires individuals to pass six tests. Of the four required exams, one is on Windows NT Workstation 3.51 or 4, two are on Windows NT Server 3.51 or 4, and the last is on Networking Essentials. The other two exams can be taken from a large pool of electives.

- **MCSE + Internet (MCSE+I)** This program aims to certify systems engineers who specialize in supporting networked environments that include an Internet presence of some type. To obtain the MCSE+I, candidates must pass nine tests. Seven of these tests are required exams, including the core four required for the MCSE plus three additional Internet-focused required exams. Two electives, which may be drawn from a fairly limited pool, are also necessary.

- **Microsoft Certified Solution Developer (MCSD)** This program aims to certify individuals who can develop custom applications for use on Microsoft networks. It requires passing four exams, as follows:

  - **Analyzing Requirements and Defining Solutions (exam 70-100)** Covers the basic Microsoft APIs and development approaches.

  - Any one of four desktop application development exams, on topics that include designing and implementing desktop applications using Visual C++, Visual Basic, Visual FoxPro, or Visual J++.

- Any one of four distributed applications development exams, on topics that include designing and implementing distributed applications using Visual C++, Visual Basic, Visual FoxPro, or Visual J++.
- Any one of a large pool of elective exams on topics as diverse as SQL Server database implementation, commerce solutions, additional programming languages, or Web applications.

Microsoft's exams are richly supported, both with official tools (built by or approved by Microsoft)—which include classroom training, self-study kits, computer-based training, books—and through a broad range of unofficial tools that cover the same types of materials. Current industry trends indicate that Microsoft certifications are the most-sought-after of any certifications; given the company's ubiquitous presence and marketing muscle, this shouldn't surprise anyone.

Novell Certification Programs

Although Microsoft may be the "800-pound gorilla" of the certification market, Novell has been at this game longer than just about anybody else, and boasts the largest population of certified professionals (400,000 plus, to Microsoft's 300,000 plus). Novell also boasts the largest installed base of any network operating system vendor.

With a major new release of its flagship product, NetWare 5, Novell's certified population will have to recertify by mid-year 2000 to remain current. This suggests an active and vigorous training and testing marketplace, and indeed, most experts expect Novell-certified professionals to actively pursue re-certification at the same time that a new generation of professionals begins its pursuit of certification around NetWare 5.

Novell currently recognizes three levels of professional certification, with various areas of specialization, plus a separate Internet certification:

- **Certified Novell Administrator (CNA)** This credential is Novell's entry-level certification. Obtaining a CNA requires passing any one of five tests that cover basic administration for three versions of NetWare (5, 4/IntranetWare, or 3), or two versions of GroupWise (5 or 4).
- **Certified Novell Engineer (CNE)** The most sought-after Novell certification is the CNE. CNEs specialize in a particular version of NetWare or GroupWise, and must pass a battery of six or seven tests (depending on which certification the individual is seeking) to qualify, including five or six required courses and one elective course. The individual must take the Network Technologies and Service and

Support tests. The remaining required exams for the NetWare CNE certification are as follows:

- **NetWare X Administration** A basic administration exam aimed at the version of NetWare for which the individual seeks certification.
- **NetWare X Advanced Administration** An advanced administration exam aimed at the version of NetWare for which the individual seeks certification.
- **NDS Administration** An exam on NetWare Directory Services (NDS) aimed at the version of NetWare for which the individual seeks certification.
- **NetWare X Installation Design and Configuration (for NetWare 3 and 4 certification only)** An installation and configuration exam aimed at the version of NetWare (3 or 4) for which the individual seeks certification.

In addition to the Networking Technologies and Service and Support tests, the remaining required exams for the GroupWise certification are as follows:

- **IntranetWare: NetWare 4.11 Administration** An administration exam aimed at NetWare 4.11/IntranetWare.
- **GroupWise X Administration** An administration exam aimed at the version of GroupWise for which the individual seeks certification.
- **GroupWise X Advanced Administration** An advanced administration exam aimed at the version of GroupWise for which the individual seeks certification.
- **GroupWise Net Access and Connectivity (for GroupWise 5 certification)** An exam on GroupWise gateways and agents; user access methods, protocols, and services; Internet access and gateways; installation; configuration; and management.
- **GroupWise 4 Async Gateway and GroupWise Remote (for GroupWise 4 certification)** A test on principles of the GroupWise 4 dial-up gateway, and use of GroupWise 4 remote access capabilities, including planning, design, installation, configuration, and management.

The electives cover topics that range from GroupWise administration to securing intranets using Novell's BorderManager product. Passing any one of these, in addition to the required exams, is what it takes to become a CNE.

- **Master CNE (MCNE)** This is Novell's most elite certification. It designates recipients as certified specialists in one of seven areas of expertise. Requirements vary from specialty to specialty, but involve anywhere from four to six tests beyond CNE certification requirements. You will learn all about these details in Chapter 3.
- **Certified Internet Professional** Working in tandem with the Association of Internet Professionals, Novell also offers a collection of certifications called Certified Internet Professional. These range from four levels of credentials from a Certified Internet Business Strategist, who must pass two exams, to a Certified Intranet Manager, who must pass five exams. For more information, please consult Chapter 3.

Even though Microsoft may appear poised to surpass Novell in terms of its certification programs' population and popularity, it's important to recognize that Novell pioneered this marketplace and that its education and certification programs have served as a model for many other vendors, including Microsoft. Even today, Novell's program is highly regarded and widely emulated. The Novell certification program is covered in detail in Chapter 3.

Oracle Certification Programs

Although Oracle might have to stretch to match Microsoft across all markets, no one can dispute its leadership in the database market. In keeping with its stature in this field, Oracle offers the Oracle Certified Professional program to certify professionals in one of two tracks:

- **Database Administrator (DBA)** This is designed for individuals who must create and maintain Oracle databases. Obtaining this credential requires passing four tests. Oracle offers a variety of training vehicles to help individuals prepare for these tests, ranging from instructor-led training to a variety of online tutorials. The four tests cover the following topics:
  - **Introduction to Oracle: SQL and PL/SQL** Covers basic database concepts and structures, plus basic programming in SQL.
  - **Oracle7.3: Oracle Database Administration** Covers database architectures, creation, and maintenance; aimed at a particular version of Oracle (currently 7.3, but version 8 is in the offing).
  - **Oracle7.3: Performance Tuning Workshop** Covers techniques for monitoring, tuning, and optimizing Oracle database and server performance; aimed at a particular version of Oracle.

- **Oracle7.3: Backup and Recovery Workshop** Covers backup and recovery tools as well as strategies for Oracle databases; also aimed at a particular version of Oracle.

- **Oracle Certified Application Developer** This is for developers who wish to establish their proficiency at developing Oracle-based applications using Oracle's Developer/2000 Release 1 development environment. Here again, Oracle offers a variety of training vehicles to help individuals prepare for the five tests required for this certification. The five tests cover the following topics:
  - **Introduction to Oracle: SQL and PL/SQL** Covers basic database concepts and structures, plus basic SQL programming.
  - **Develop PL/SQL Program Units** Covers developing and managing stored procedures, functions, packages, and database triggers.
  - **Developer/2000 Forms 4.5 I** Covers using Developer/2000 tools and environment, plus basic forms development, including forms editors, modules, blocks, events, and more.
  - **Developer/2000 Forms 4.5 II** Covers advanced forms development, including menu modules, function keys, managing windows and canvases, manipulating forms at runtime, and more.
  - **Developer/2000 Reports 2.5** Covers programming for Oracle's report generator, including designing, using, and maintaining reports, plus managing data models, layouts, parameters, triggers, and more.

Given that most Oracle installations cost upwards of half a million dollars, training and certification are quite customary in this environment (and often, training and consulting services are negotiated as part of an overall purchase agreement). As a result, certification is a key ingredient for hiring new database professionals, and for ensuring that current employees maintain their skills. You'll learn more about Oracle Certified Professional exams, training, and resources in Chapter 4.

Cisco Certification Programs

Although less than 5,000 individuals currently hold some type of Cisco certification, this company's programs currently enjoy terrific cachet. This is primarily because Cisco Career Certifications are so scarce, and their services are in such high demand, that elite Cisco Career Certification candidates can expect to make six-figure incomes immediately upon obtaining their credentials. With a potential payday of this magnitude, this certification is the current hot ticket.

The buzz aside, there are plenty of other good reasons why those with a Cisco certification are in high demand. As the leading purveyor of routing, switching, and connectivity equipment, Cisco dominates the markets for Internet and intranet gear. Because its equipment and software are both sophisticated and powerful, certification is viewed as essential for those individuals entrusted to work on such mission-critical systems and software.

Cisco offers multiple certifications, each of which may be obtained across three different disciplines. All three of the disciplines require a strong general background in networking technologies and concepts, but each represents a specialized area of focus:

- **Routing and Switching** This discipline covers the use of routers and switches in enterprise-level internetworks, and includes coverage of WAN technologies only insofar as they tie into organizational networks.
- **ISP Dial** This focuses on the kinds of internetworking issues more typical at an Internet Service Provider—namely, some coverage of routers and switches, but also of telephony, modems and other remote communications devices, Web and Internet security issues, and communications servers.
- **WAN Switching** This discipline covers the long-haul aspects of WAN communications, and includes coverage of routers and switches, a wide variety of WAN link technologies, voice/data/video integration, plus Internet security issues.

Across these three disciplines, Cisco offers various certifications. Of the five in the following list, the first three represent a certification ladder for individuals who take an operating role in building and maintaining internetworks that incorporate Cisco components. The final two represent a certification ladder for those who seek to design and deploy such internetworks.

> **TIP** Typically, individuals would climb the first ladder at an organization that uses or operates such a network. Individuals would climb the second ladder at a consulting company or other organization that specializes in building and deploying networks for third parties.

Together, these five certifications include the following:

- **Cisco Certified Network Associate (CCNA)** This is the entry-level operational certification and is aimed at individuals who must manage simple routed LANs or WANs, small ISPs, or smaller switch LAN or LANE environments. Passing a single multiple-choice exam is required to obtain this certification.

- **Cisco Certified Network Professional (CCNP)** This is the middle-tier operational certification, aimed at individuals who must install, configure, operate and troubleshoot complex routed LANs, routed WANs, switch LAN networks, or Dial Access Services. Applicants must first obtain a CCNA, and then take either two or four additional exams, depending on which test options they choose.
- **Cisco Certified Internetwork Expert (CCIE)** This is the top-tier operational certification, aimed at individuals who have advanced technical skills and knowledge, who know how to configure networks for optimum performance, and who understand how to maintain complex, far-flung, multivendor networks. Applicants must pass only two exams for this certification: a written exam through normal channels and a laboratory evaluation at one of Cisco's certification labs.

Cisco's lab exams have the reputation of being the most challenging and difficult certification tests in the networking industry, bar none. In addition to their difficulty, the Cisco required lab exams are also the most expensive certification exams around. They are offered only at a small number of locations, and usually involve travel expenses beyond the cost of the exam itself ($1,000).

- **Cisco Certified Design Associate (CCDA)** This is the entry-level design credential. It requires individuals to be able to design and deploy simple routed and switched networks, as well as configure, operate, and maintain them. To obtain this certification, applicants must pass a single exam (9E0-004). (This certification is not an option for those seeking WAN Switching specialization.)
- **Cisco Certified Design Professional (CCDP)** This is the top-tier design credential. It requires individuals to be able to design and deploy complex routed LANs and WANs, plus switched LANs and LANE environments. Likewise, individuals must be able to configure, operate, and maintain such networks and connections. For those seeking the Routing and Switching or ISP Dial specialty, applications must first obtain CCNA and CCDA certification, and then pass either two or four exams, depending on which exam track they elect. For those seeking the WAN Switching specialty, they must first obtain CCNP certification and then take one additional test.

You'll learn more about the requirements and expertise required for all Cisco certifications in Chapter 5.

CompTIA's A+ Certification Program

CompTIA stands for the Computing Technology Industry Association. Its members include most major PC hardware and software manufacturers. This organization offers the A+ certification to provide vendor-neutral credentials for PC technicians who are able to handle a broad variety of hardware, operating systems, and related matters.

A new exam, called Network+ (slated for delivery in spring 1999), will aim to provide similar, vendor-neutral credentials for network technicians (who seldom work in single-vendor environments, in any case).

Obtaining A+ certification requires passing two exams:

- **Core** Focuses on basic principles of computer operation, configuration, installation, and maintenance. The purpose of this test is to examine a candidate's knowledge and understanding of computer systems, peripherals, and components.
- **DOS/Windows** Focuses on installation, configuration, maintenance, and troubleshooting of DOS and Windows (through Windows 95) operating systems. The purpose of this test is to examine a candidate's knowledge and understanding of the basic desktop PC operating systems and services.

Unlike the certification programs previously mentioned, CompTIA requires that both tests be taken and passed within a 90-day period. Otherwise, candidates must retake both tests to obtain A+ certification. You'll learn more about the details and requirements for this widely held computer certification in Chapter 6.

SunSoft's Java Certification Programs

Given the immense popularity of Java as a programming language, it should come as no surprise that SunSoft (the subsidiary of Sun Microsystems, Inc., that's responsible for developing and promoting this technology) has instituted a Java certification program.

Currently, about 10,000 individuals have obtained one level of Java certification or another, and a great many more are expected to complete certification by the end of 1999. As companies like IBM and Sun Microsystems undertake new development work in Java, and seek to convert existing code to Java, demand for qualified Java programmers is exploding. Certified Java professionals are not as pricey as Cisco professionals, although they can certainly command a premium in today's marketplace.

SunSoft offers two levels of Java certification:

- **Certified Java Programmer** Individuals who seek this certification must take a written test aimed at a specific Java Development Kit (JDK). The most current test covers JDK 1.1, and another is available on the JDK 1.0.2; a new test is expected by the end of 1998 on JDK 1.2. Individuals who take this test must be familiar with basic Java language constructs and concepts, and intimately familiar with the APIs and tools in the JDK.
- **Certified Java Developer** Individuals who seek this certification must submit an application and pay a fee to receive a set of specifications for a full-blown Java application. They must then create an application to meet the specifications, and submit it to SunSoft for evaluation. Following a critique and analysis of their work, applicants who pass must successfully implement all the basic requirements of the specification they receive. Individuals who take this test must first pass the Certified Java Programmer test, and be familiar enough with Java programming and development techniques to complete their assignment. The amount of work involved is usually between two and five days—according to those who have taken this test.

Sun offers classroom training and an online tutorial to help individuals prepare for this test. If you've spent any time in a bookstore with a decent selection of computer titles lately, you're probably aware that books on Java constitute a heavily populated niche in the computer section. There is no lack of information or documentation available to those who seek this certification. For more details about Sun's programs and offerings, please consult Chapter 7.

Summary

This concludes our overview of the various vendor and organization certifications that you'll encounter in this book. The remainder of this book is devoted to more detailed descriptions and discussions of their programs, exams, and supporting materials. Enjoy!

Need To Know More?

This book includes a companion CD that provides additional material about the various certification programs I mention throughout this book. Be sure to check it out!

www.microsoft.com/train_cert/ This is the "mother of all Web pages" for topics and information related to Microsoft certification. Be sure to investigate the buttons on the left-hand side of this home page; Find An Exam and Certification Choices are particularly useful.

http://services.novell.com/ This is a good point of departure to investigate Novell's certification programs, exams, and training options, all of which may be located under the Learn Faster heading at the top right on the page.

http://education.oracle.com/certification/ This is where you can begin your investigation of Oracle's certification programs, exams, and training. Be prepared to read a lot of PDF files as you peruse its thorough, but fragmented, documents and descriptions.

www.cisco.com/warp/public/10/wwtraining/certprog/ This page describes Cisco's certifications in general, with pointers to other pages with details on courses, examinations, requirements, and all types of other useful stuff. Cisco's online information is the only instance where I found lists of recommended reading and online resources to help individuals prepare for the tests, for which Cisco is due considerable kudos!

www.comptia.org Follow pointers to the A+ or Network+ certifications to learn more about these tests and their background requirements.

http://suned.sun.com/usa/cert_test.html This is where you can begin your investigation of SunSoft's certification programs, exams, and training.

2

Microsoft Certification Programs

Terms you'll need to understand:

- √ MCP, MCP+I, MCP+SB, MCSE, MCSE+I, MCSD, MOUS
- √ Windows product family: Windows 95, Windows 98, Windows NT
- √ System or network administrator
- √ Software developer
- √ Microsoft exam IDs

Techniques you'll need to master:

- √ Locating training and certification information on the Microsoft Web site
- √ Obtaining descriptions and objectives for specific Microsoft exams
- √ Locating practice tests to help you prepare for specific Microsoft exams

Of all the vendor programs you'll encounter in this book, Microsoft's certification programs are arguably the most varied. Definitely, no other vendor whose programs are covered in this book offers as many different exams (not to mention related classroom training, courseware, self-study kits, and books) as Microsoft does. In this chapter, you'll have a chance to examine Microsoft's many different certification options, and to understand how one certification can sometimes lead to another.

Alphabet Soup

To begin with, let's review the many acronyms that relate to certification, Microsoft style. After that, you'll have a chance to investigate each certification in some detail. Then, you'll be presented with a roadmap that shows how all the pieces fit together, and learn how to sign up for tests, track certification progress, and so on.

Here's the list of key acronyms related to Microsoft certifications, with brief explanations for each one:

- **Microsoft Certified Professional (MCP)** Anyone who's passed any one exam on a current Microsoft application or operating system.
- **MCP + Internet (MCP+I)** MCP candidates who prove their Internet expertise, and qualify to plan security, installation, and configuration of server products; implement server extensions; and manage server resources. Three core exams are required to pass.
- **MCP + Site Building (MCP+SB)** MCP candidates who prove their expertise in managing sophisticated, interactive Web sites, including databases, multimedia, and searchable content. To qualify, candidates must pass two of three required exams.
- **Microsoft Certified Systems Engineer (MCSE)** Candidates who prove their expertise with desktop and server operating systems, networking components, and Microsoft BackOffice products. To qualify, candidates must pass six exams—four core exams and two electives.
- **MCSE + Internet (MCSE+I)** MCSE candidates who prove their expertise using Microsoft products and technologies in Internet or intranet environments. As with the basic MCSE, candidates must pass the same core four MCSE exams, plus three Internet core exams, and two Internet-specific electives.
- **Microsoft Certified Solution Developer (MCSD)** Candidates who prove their abilities to build Web-based, distributed, or e-commerce

applications. This program is aimed at developers rather than system or network managers. Knowledge of solution architectures, application-development strategies and techniques, and development tools is required of all candidates, who must pass three core exams and one elective exam to qualify.

- **Microsoft Office User Specialist (MOUS)** Office workers such as temps, administrators, and clerical staff who prove their abilities to handle the Microsoft Office productivity suite (which includes Word, Excel, Access, and PowerPoint) in either the Office 95 or Office 97 versions. This program recognizes three levels of certification: a Proficient Specialist for Word and Excel, Expert Specialist for each of the Office components, and Microsoft Office Expert for those who are experts in all Office components and who pass an integration test to boot.

All the information in the preceding list, plus some additional details about the exams, is summed up in Table 2.1. Please note that information about the number of questions, the cost, and the time period is for each exam, not for all exams.

In the sections that follow, you'll examine each of these certifications in some detail, and learn a little more about the exams that you must pass to qualify for each one. If you visit the URLs mentioned for each credential, in most cases you'll be able to jump straight to the details related to the required exams (and electives, where applicable).

STUDY ALERT: Microsoft is now administering some MCP exams in the adaptive test format. Table 2.1 contains information about fixed-length exams. The number of questions and time allowed will vary for adaptive exams. See the section titled "Microsoft Testing" for more information.

Table 2.1 Microsoft certifications, exams, and more.

Certification	Required Exams	Elective Exams	Questions	Cost	Time
MCP	1	0	50-70	$100	70-90 min.
MCP+I	3	0	50-70	$100	70-90 min.
MCP+SB	2	0	50-70	$100	70-90 min.
MCSE	4	2	50-70	$100	70-90 min.
MCSE+I	7	2	50-70	$100	70-90 min.
MCSD	3	1	50-70	$100	70-90 min.
MOUS	1-5	0	50-60	$50	30-60 min.

MCP

Anyone who passes any Microsoft certification exam—other than exam 70-058, Networking Essentials, or any of the Office-related exams—can become certified as an MCP. Because you will learn about the range of exams that this broad category includes in the following sections, I will not list them here.

For a more detailed description of the requirements to become an MCP, visit Microsoft's MCP page at **www.microsoft.com/mcp/certstep/mcps.htm**. For a step-by-step guide to obtaining MCP credentials, visit **www.microsoft.com/mcp/certstep/steps.htm**.

MCP+I

MCPs who want to specialize in Internet tools and technologies must pass three exams to demonstrate their technical proficiency and expertise. Microsoft designs these exams based on input from industry professionals, and they are intended to reflect how Microsoft products are used in a business or organizational setting.

Individuals who obtain MCP+I certification are assumed to be qualified to plan Internet and network security, to install and configure Windows NT Server products, and to manage related resources. They should also be able to extend NT-based Web servers to run Common Gateway Interface (CGI) or Internet Server API (ISAPI) scripts, monitor and analyze server performance, or troubleshoot problems. Table 2.2 summarizes the requirements for obtaining MCP+I certification.

For more information about this certification, please visit Microsoft's Web page at **www.microsoft.com/mcp/certstep/internet.htm**.

MCP+SB

The MCP+SB credential is aimed primarily at Web site developers who seek to demonstrate their knowledge of related Microsoft tools and technologies. Individuals who hold the MCP+SB certification are judged to be qualified to build, maintain, and manage Web sites using Microsoft products and technologies. This credential will be of greatest value to those who manage complex, interactive Web sites that integrate a variety of content types (such as multimedia and database access) and that include searchable content. Requirements for obtaining an MCP+SB are covered in Table 2.3; to qualify, you need only pass any two of the three exams that are listed.

For more information about obtaining an MCP+SB, please visit **www.microsoft.com/mcp/certstep/mcp_sb.htm**.

Table 2.2 The MCP+I exams.

Exam ID and Title	70-059	Internetworking with Microsoft TCP/IP on Microsoft Windows NT 4.0
Description		Covers NT 4 TCP/IP protocols, addressing, subnets, DNS, WINS, plus services and utilities.
Exam ID and Title	70-067	Implementing and Supporting Microsoft Windows NT Server 4.0
Description		Covers basic Windows NT Server 4 planning, installation, configuration, and management.
Exam ID and Title	70-077	Implementing and Supporting Microsoft IIS 3.0 and Microsoft Index Server 1.1
OR		
Exam ID and Title	70-087	Implementing and Supporting Microsoft IIS 4.0
Description		70-077 covers IIS 3 and Index Server 1.1 and 70-087 covers the current version. In either case, you must know how to install, configure, and maintain IIS and Index Server, and understand security, content management, Web site design, and related IP services.

Table 2.3 The MCP+SB exams.

Choose any two of the following three exams.		
Exam ID and Title	70-055	Designing and Implementing Web Sites with Microsoft FrontPage 98
Description		Covers FrontPage tools and utilities; Web site design, deployment, and maintenance; and extending Web site functionality and interactivity using FrontPage 98.
Exam ID and Title	70-057	Designing and Implementing Commerce Solutions with Microsoft Site Server 3.0, Commerce Edition
Description		Covers designing, implementing, managing, and securing an e-commerce presence on the Web, and using Site Server 3 and its various commerce tools and extensions.
Exam ID and Title	70-152	Designing and Implementing Web Solutions with Microsoft Visual InterDev 6.0
Description		Covers working with Microsoft's Visual development toolset for building Web extensions, including CGI programs, ISAPI programs, ActiveX controls, Active Server Pages, and so on.

MCSE

The MCSE credential is the most widely sought-after of all the Microsoft certifications. Individuals who attain this status must pass four core exams and two electives. Of the four core exams, two cover one of Microsoft's server platforms (NT Server 3.51 or NT Server 4), one covers a desktop operating system (you have three choices, as shown in Table 2.4), and the last is the Networking Essentials exam. The two electives may be drawn from a broad range of choices, as shown in Table 2.5.

The goal that drives the MCSE is to create a class of professionals who are at home working with Microsoft's desktop and server operating systems, but who also understand how to design, implement, and maintain a modern network. In short, an MCSE is judged to be capable of planning, designing, and

Table 2.4 The MCSE required core exams: Microsoft Windows NT 4 track.

Exam ID and Title	70-067	Implementing and Supporting Microsoft Windows NT Server 4.0
Description		Covers basic Windows NT 4 Server planning, installation, configuration, and management.
Exam ID and Title	70-068	Implementing and Supporting Microsoft Windows NT Server 4.0 in the Enterprise
Description		Covers advanced configuration and management topics aimed at large-scale enterprise-level networks and installations.
Exam ID and Title	70-058	Networking Essentials
Description		Covers basic networking concepts, terminology, and concepts, and design and operation of LANs and WANs.
Exam ID and Title	70-064	Implementing and Supporting Microsoft Windows 95
OR		
Exam ID and Title	70-073	Implementing and Supporting Microsoft Windows NT Workstation 4.0
OR		
Exam ID and Title	70-098	Implementing and Supporting Microsoft Windows 98
Description		These tests cover each desktop operating system's features and functions, as well as how to install, configure, and administer them on a network, both locally and remotely.

Table 2.5 MCSE elective exams.

Choose any two items in this list, except for entries separated by the keyword **OR**, which indicates only one of the items in that category may be counted as an MCSE elective.

Exam ID and Title	70-013	Implementing and Supporting Microsoft SNA Server 3.0
OR		
Exam ID and Title	70-085	Implementing and Supporting Microsoft SNA Server 4.0
Description		Both tests cover Microsoft's IBM mainframe connectivity servers. Topics include terminal emulation, host sessions, LAN-to-host data transfer, and so on.
Exam ID and Title	70-018	Implementing and Supporting Microsoft Systems Management Server 1.2
OR		
Exam ID and Title	70-086	Implementing and Supporting Microsoft Systems Management Server 2.0
Description		Both tests cover Microsoft's BackOffice network management toolset, and deal with topics including remote management, software distribution, network monitoring and management, and so on.
Exam ID and Title	70-027	Implementing a Database Design on Microsoft SQL Server 6.5
OR		
Exam ID and Title	70-029	Implementing a Database Design on Microsoft SQL Server 7.0
Description		Both tests cover Microsoft's BackOffice database engine, and deal with topics including database design, testing, and deployment.
Exam ID and Title	70-026	System Administration for Microsoft SQL Server 6.5
OR		
Exam ID and Title	70-028	Administering Microsoft SQL Server 7.0
Description		Both tests cover Microsoft's BackOffice database engine, and deal with what happens when design and deployment leave off—namely, database maintenance, programming, migration, and troubleshooting.
Exam ID and Title	70-059	Internetworking with Microsoft TCP/IP on Microsoft Windows NT 4.0
Description		Covers NT 4 TCP/IP protocols, addressing, subnets, DNS, WINS, plus services and utilities.
Exam ID and Title	70-056	Implementing and Supporting Web Sites Using Microsoft Site Server 3.0
Description		Covers Microsoft's BackOffice intranet information-delivery environment. Topics include how to publish information, search for information, and deliver information to users via email, channels, or Web pages.

(continued)

Table 2.5 MCSE elective exams *(continued)*.

Exam ID and Title	70-076	Implementing and Supporting Microsoft Exchange Server 5
OR		
Exam ID and Title	70-081	Implementing and Supporting Microsoft Exchange Server 5.5
Description		Both exams cover Microsoft BackOffice's messaging engine, and deal with topics that include design and deployment of email systems, Internet links, messaging-based applications, and so on. These are regarded as among the hardest of the exams.
Exam ID and Title	70-077	Implementing and Supporting Microsoft IIS 3.0 and Microsoft Index Server 1.1
OR		
Exam ID and Title	70-087	Implementing and Supporting Microsoft IIS 4.0
Description		70-077 covers IIS 3 and Index Server 1.1; 70-087 covers the current version. In either case, you must know how to install, configure, and maintain IIS and Index Server, and understand security, content management, Web site design, and related IP services.
Exam ID and Title	70-078	Implementing and Supporting Microsoft Proxy Server 1.0
OR		
Exam ID and Title	70-088	Implementing and Supporting Microsoft Proxy Server 2.0
Description		70-078 covers Proxy Server 1; 70-088 covers the current version. For both exams, topics include maintaining intranet security using Proxy Server, packet and address filtering and exceptions, managing protocols, and working with related tools and utilities.

implementing business information systems around networks, and to deal with the supplementary technologies that operate in such environments, particularly those found in Microsoft's BackOffice family of products.

As of this writing, Microsoft also offers a Windows NT 3.51 track for the MCSE, as well as operating system exams on Windows 3.1 and Windows For Workgroups 3.11. However, all of these items are scheduled to be retired in the relatively near future. For more information on these older programs, visit the URL listed at the end of this section.

Note that as of this writing, Microsoft also offers numerous other exams that still qualify as valid electives. However, all of the items that do not appear in Table 2.5 are scheduled to be retired in the relatively near future. For more information on these older programs, please visit Microsoft's MSCE Web page at **www.microsoft.com/mcp/certstep/mcse.htm**.

MCSE+I

Although the plain-vanilla MCSE might be the most sought-after Microsoft certification, MCSE+I is certainly the most demanding. It requires passing nine exams: the core four required for the regular MCSE, three additional core exams (most of which are valid electives for a plain MCSE), and two Internet-specific electives. The MCSE+I credential adds to the ordinary MCSE's understanding of internal systems and networks, a thorough knowledge and appreciation of the tools, products, and problems that one is likely to encounter when working with the Internet.

Rather than repeating all the information from the MCSE section, Table 2.6 lists only the additional core requirements for MCSE+I. Likewise, the electives for MCSE+I are listed in Table 2.7. Please note that only the Windows NT 4 track applies to MSCE+I; that certification does not accept the 3.51 Windows NT track for its core four requirements.

For more information about the MSCE+I credentials and requirements, visit **www.microsoft.com/mcp/certstep/mcsein.htm.**

Table 2.6 Additional MCSE+I required core exams.

In addition to the tests listed in this table, you must also meet the Windows NT 4 core four requirements for the regular MCSE, as described in Table 2.4.

Exam ID and Title	70-059	Internetworking with Microsoft TCP/IP on Microsoft Windows NT 4.0
Description		Covers NT 4 TCP/IP protocols, addressing, subnets, DNS, WINS, plus services and utilities.
Exam ID and Title	70-077	Implementing and Supporting Microsoft IIS 3.0 and Microsoft Index Server 1.1
OR		
Exam ID and Title	70-087	Implementing and Supporting Microsoft IIS 4.0
Description		70-077 covers IIS 3 and Index Server 1.1; 70-087 covers the current version. In either case, you must know how to install, configure, and maintain IIS and Index Server, and understand security, content management, Web site design, and related IP services.
Exam ID and Title	70-079	Implementing and Supporting Microsoft Internet Explorer 4.0 by Using the Internet Explorer Administration Kit
Description		Covers planning, deployment, configuration, and automated installation of IE 4 on multiple desktops using Microsoft's IEAK, including channel design and delivery, desktop customization, and so on.

Table 2.7 MCSE+I elective exams.

Choose any two items in this list, except for entries separated by the keyword **OR**, which indicates only one of the items in that category may be counted as an MCSE+I elective.

Exam ID and Title	70-026	Administering Microsoft SQL Server 6.5
OR		
Exam ID and Title	70-028	Administering Microsoft SQL Server 7.0
Description		Both tests cover Microsoft's BackOffice database engine, and deal with what happens when design and deployment leave off—namely, database maintenance, programming, migration, and troubleshooting.
Exam ID and Title	70-027	Implementing a Database Design on Microsoft SQL Server 6.5
OR		
Exam ID and Title	70-029	Implementing a Database Design on Microsoft SQL Server 7.0
Description		Both tests cover Microsoft's BackOffice database engine, and deal with topics including database design, testing, and deployment.
Exam ID and Title	70-056	Implementing and Supporting Web Sites Using Microsoft Site Server 3.0
Description		Covers Microsoft's BackOffice intranet information-delivery environment. Topics include how to publish information, search for information, and deliver information to users via email, channels, or Web pages.
Exam ID and Title	70-076	Implementing and Supporting Microsoft Exchange Server 5
OR		
Exam ID and Title	70-081	Implementing and Supporting Microsoft Exchange Server 5.5
Description		Both exams cover Microsoft BackOffice's messaging engine, and deal with topics that include design and deployment of email systems, Internet links, messaging-based applications, and so on. Regarded as among the hardest of the exams.
Exam ID and Title	70-078	Implementing and Supporting Microsoft Proxy Server 1.0
OR		
Exam ID and Title	70-088	Implementing and Supporting Microsoft Proxy Server 2.0
Description		70-078 covers Proxy Server 1; 70-088 covers the current version. For both exams, topics include maintaining intranet security using Proxy Server, packet and address filtering and exceptions, managing protocols, and working with related tools and utilities.
Exam ID and Title	70-085	Implementing and Supporting Microsoft SNA Server 4.0
Description		Covers Microsoft's IBM mainframe connectivity servers. Topics include terminal emulation, host sessions, LAN-to-host data transfer, IP connectivity, and so on.

MCSD

The MCSD credential is aimed at software developers who seek to construct business solutions using Microsoft development tools, technologies, and platforms. As a result, this particular program has very little overlap with those you've examined so far in this chapter. MCPs and MCSEs may design and build systems around specific Microsoft components and products; however, if they develop content, its software component is more incidental or supplementary rather than central. But for MCSDs, building or customizing software solutions is assumed to be their primary activity.

MCSDs are required to pass three core exams and one elective exam. The core technology exams require candidates to demonstrate their competence with Microsoft's solution architecture, and with developing desktop and distributed applications. The elective exams allow individuals to use their knowledge of programming languages or development environments. Table 2.8 lists the core requirements for the MCSD; Table 2.9 lists the electives.

Because there are so many electives for the MCSD, and nearly all of them have been covered elsewhere in this chapter, I will forgo the brief description that has accompanied exam listings up to this point. Please consult the URL at the end of this section for easy access to details on all the exams that appear in Table 2.9.

Please note that the MCSD requirements outlined in Table 2.9 replace an older set of requirements that have recently been retired. If you've already completed those elements of the older testing regimen, you may still be able to certify under that old program. For more information about this older program, and the tests mentioned in Table 2.9, please visit **www.microsoft.com/mcp/certstep/mscd.htm**.

Table 2.8 MCSD required core exams.		
Desktop Applications Requirement (choose any one of the following)		
Exam ID and Title	70-016	Designing and Implementing Desktop Applications with Microsoft Visual C++ 6.0
Exam ID and Title	70-176	Designing and Implementing Desktop Applications with Microsoft Visual Basic 6.0
Exam ID and Title	70-XXX	Designing and Implementing Desktop Applications with Microsoft Visual FoxPro (to be released in 1999)
Exam ID and Title	70-XXX	Designing and Implementing Desktop Applications with Microsoft Visual J++ (to be released In 1999)

(continued)

Table 2.8 MCSD required core exams *(continued)*.		
Distributed Applications Requirement (choose any one of the following)		
Exam ID and Title	70-015	Designing and Implementing Distributed Applications with Microsoft Visual C++ 6.0
Exam ID and Title	70-175	Designing and Implementing Distributed Applications with Microsoft Visual Basic 6.0
Exam ID and Title	70-XXX	Designing and Implementing Distributed Applications with Microsoft Visual FoxPro (to be released in 1999)
Exam ID and Title	70-XXX	Designing and Implementing Distributed Applications with Microsoft Visual J++ (to be released in 1999)
Solution Architecture Requirement		
Exam ID and Title	70-100	Analyzing Requirements and Defining Solution Architectures
Description		Covers Microsoft's application planning, design, and implementation tools and strategies; also includes coverage of all important Microsoft APIs and development models (of which there are many). This is regarded as one of the toughest Microsoft exams.

Table 2.9 MCSD elective exams.		
Choose any item in this list, except for entries separate by the keyword **OR**, which indicates only one of the items in that category may be counted as an MCSD elective.		
Exam ID and Title	70-015	Designing and Implementing Distributed Applications with Microsoft Visual C++ 6.0
Exam ID and Title	70-016	Designing and Implementing Desktop Applications with Microsoft Visual C++ 6.0
Exam ID and Title **OR** **Exam ID and Title**	70-027 70-029	Implementing a Database Design on Microsoft SQL Server 6.5 Implementing a Database Design on Microsoft SQL Server 7.0
Exam ID and Title	70-024	Developing Applications with C++ Using the Microsoft Foundation Class Library
Exam ID and Title	70-025	Implementing OLE in Microsoft Foundation Class Applications
Exam ID and Title	70-055	Designing and Implementing Web Sites with Microsoft FrontPage 98
Exam ID and Title	70-057	Designing and Implementing Commerce Solutions with Microsoft Site Server 3.0, Commerce Edition

(continued)

Table 2.9 MCSD elective exams *(continued)*.

Exam ID and Title	70-165	Developing Applications with Microsoft Visual Basic 5.0
OR		
Exam ID and Title	70-175	Designing and Implementing Distributed Applications with Microsoft Visual Basic 6.0
OR		
Exam ID and Title	70-176	Designing and Implementing Desktop Applications with Microsoft Visual Basic 6.0
Exam ID and Title	70-069	Application Development with Microsoft Access for Windows 95 and the Microsoft Access Developer's Toolkit
Exam ID and Title	70-091	Designing and Implementing Solutions with Microsoft Office 2000 and Microsoft Visual Basic for Applications
Exam ID and Title	70-152	Designing and Implementing Web Solutions with Microsoft Visual InterDev 6.0
(Note that a Database Design exam for Access is scheduled for 1999 release.)		

MOUS

The MOUS program is designed to provide a cadre of certified individuals who can function in today's workplace. Because the skills that an MOUS can document are in such high demand, Microsoft has announced that it intends to ensure that over one million individuals obtain some level of MOUS certification by the end of 1999.

The MOUS program recognizes three levels of proficiency, as follows:

- **Microsoft Office Proficient Specialist** This level indicates that users can handle a wide range of everyday tasks, and requires working knowledge of both Microsoft Word and Microsoft Excel (95 or 97 versions).
- **Microsoft Office Expert Specialist** This level indicates that users can handle complex assignments that involve advanced formatting and functionality. This certification applies to any of the four primary components of Office 97 (Word, Excel, PowerPoint, and Access), and includes other products in the MS Office family, such as FrontPage. Thus, an individual could claim to be a Microsoft Expert Specialist in Excel and Word, for instance.
- **Microsoft Office Expert** This level indicates that users have attained Expert Specialist status in all five of the Office 97 components for which testing is currently available: Word, Excel, PowerPoint, Access, and FrontPage. This is the highest-level MOUS certification available.

Unlike other Microsoft tests mentioned so far in this chapter, MOUS tests rely almost entirely on simulation techniques and task-oriented assignments to assess the test-taker's skills. That is, most of the questions involve manipulating a mock-up of one or more Office applications' interfaces, and require individuals to complete a battery of assignments within a period of time.

At present, no details about the names and numbers for the MOUS tests are available. Please check the following URL for more information: **www.microsoft.com/office/train_cert/**. Based on the descriptions of the MOUS program currently available, however, I expect to see six tests announced in the near future: one for the Office Proficient Specialist, and one each for the five Office components for which Office Expert Specialist status will be available (Word, Excel, PowerPoint, Access, and FrontPage).

Microsoft Testing

By now, you've certainly read about a sizable number of Microsoft tests. You are probably wondering what's involved in signing up for or taking such tests. Nothing could be easier than to explain how this process works!

For all the MCP, MCSE, and MCSD tests, you may sign up with one of two testing companies that handle testing for Microsoft certification:

- **Sylvan Prometric** You can sign up for a test through the company's Web site (current exams only, no beta exams through the Web) at **www.slspro.com/msreg/microsof.asp**. Or, you can register by phone at 1-800-755-EXAM (within the United States or Canada) or at 410-843-8000 (outside the United States and Canada).
- **Virtual University Enterprises** You can sign up for a test or get the phone numbers for local testing centers through the Web page at **www.microsoft.com/train_cert/mcp/vue_info.htm**.

To sign up for a test, you must possess a valid credit card, or contact either company for mailing instructions to send them a check (in the U.S.). You can register for a test only when payment is verified or a check has cleared.

To schedule an exam, call or visit either of the Web pages that appear in the preceding list at least one day in advance. To cancel or reschedule an exam, you must call at least 12 hours before the scheduled test time (or you may be charged, even if you don't appear to take the test). When you want to schedule a test, please have the following information ready:

- Your name, organization, and mailing address.
- Your Microsoft Test ID. (Inside the United States, this means your social security number; citizens of other nations should call ahead to find out what type of identification number is required to register for a test.)
- The name and number of the exam you wish to take.
- A method of payment.

Once you sign up for a test, you'll be informed as to when and where the test is scheduled. Try to arrive at least 15 minutes early. You must supply two forms of identification, one of which must be a photo ID.

All Microsoft exams are closed book. In fact, you will not be allowed to take anything with you into the testing area; you will be furnished with a blank sheet of paper and a pen. I suggest that you immediately write down whatever you've memorized for the test before you actually begin to take the test. You will have some time to compose yourself and to record this information.

As of this writing, Microsoft is moving away from fixed-length exams and developing adaptive exams, which are designed to determine the candidate's testing level. Despite the fact that the subject matter on which you are tested is the same, fixed-length and adaptive exams vary in the number of questions and the time limit. In adaptive testing, the number of questions each individual answers depends on the number of correct or incorrect responses. Candidates are given a different question following an incorrect answer than they would be given if the question was answered correctly. Therefore, you cannot mark a question and come back to answer it later, as you can on fixed-length tests. For more information, visit the Microsoft site at **www.microsoft.com/mcp/articles/tesinn.htm**.

To sign up for a MOUS test, you must identify a local MOUS testing center, and call it directly to schedule the test you want to take. At present, this means calling one of the two numbers that follow to identify which testing center to call:

- 800-933-4493 in North America
- #0800 973 031 or #0345 002 000 in the United Kingdom

Elsewhere, call Microsoft's main number at 425-882-8080, and ask to be connected to a Microsoft Office User Specialist program coordinator. Expect most of the financial terms and restrictions to be like those I've described for the other Microsoft tests earlier in this section.

Tracking MCP Status

As soon as you pass any Microsoft operating system exam, you'll attain MCP status. Microsoft also generates transcripts that indicate the exams you have passed and your corresponding test scores. You can order a transcript by email by sending an email to **mcp@msprograms.com**. You can also obtain a copy of your transcript by calling the Microsoft Certified Professional program's customer service number at 800-636-7544 in North America. Outside North America, please contact the Microsoft location nearest you for more information.

Becoming An MCSE

Once you pass the necessary set of six exams, you'll be certified as an MCSE. Official notification normally takes anywhere from four to six weeks, so don't expect to get your credentials overnight. When the package arrives, it will include a Welcome Kit that contains a number of elements, including:

- An MCSE certificate, suitable for framing, along with an MCSE Professional Program membership card and lapel pin.
- A license to use the MCP logo, thereby allowing you to use the logo in advertisements, promotions, documents, on letterhead, business cards, and so on. An MCP logo sheet, which includes camera-ready artwork, comes with the license. (Note that before using any of the artwork, individuals must sign and return a licensing agreement that indicates they'll abide by its terms and conditions.)
- A one-year subscription to TechNet—a collection of CDs that includes software, documentation, service packs, databases, and more technical information than you can digest in a month. In my mind, access to TechNet is the best and most tangible benefit of attaining MCSE status.
- A subscription to *Microsoft Certified Professional* magazine, which provides ongoing data about testing and certification activities, requirements, and changes to the program.
- A one-year subscription to the Microsoft Beta Evaluation program. This subscription gets you all Microsoft beta products for the next year. (This does not include developer products. You must join the Microsoft Developer Network [MSDN] program or become an MCSD to qualify for developer beta products.)

Many people believe that the benefits of MCSE certification go well beyond the perks that Microsoft provides to newly anointed members of this elite group. I'm starting to see more job listings that request or require applicants to have an

MCSE, and many individuals who complete the program can qualify for increases in pay and/or responsibility. As an official recognition of hard work and broad knowledge, MCSE certification is a badge of honor in many IT organizations. Likewise, the same is true of MCSE+I and MCSD certifications.

Tracking MOUS Status

At present, Microsoft hasn't yet automated access to MOUS status and test results as it has for its other certifications (I expect that to change before the end of 1999, however, given Microsoft's ambitious recruitment objectives). Right now, you must call one of the following phone numbers to locate a testing center near you, or to obtain MOUS status information:

- 800-933-4493 in North America
- #0800 973 031 or #0345 002 000 in the United Kingdom

Elsewhere, call Microsoft's main number at 425-882-8080 and ask to speak with a Microsoft Office User Specialist program coordinator.

How To Prepare For A Microsoft Exam

At a minimum, you should use the following to prepare for a Microsoft exam:

- For most exams, Microsoft offers self-study kits or computer trade books. Microsoft Press publishes both types of materials. You can search for such information using the search facilities at your favorite online bookstore, or at the Microsoft Press site at **http://mspress.microsoft.com**.
- Exam preparation materials, practice tests, and self-assessment exams are available for most, if not all, tests on the Microsoft Training And Certification Downloads page (**www.microsoft.com/train_cert/download/downld.htm**). Find these materials, download them, and use them!
- Check out Certification Insider Press's *Exam Cram* and *Exam Prep* books. The *Exam Cram*s are the first and last things you should read before taking an exam. They are complete with practice questions, study tips, additional resources, and a sample test. *Exam Prep*s are detailed study guides to help those not already familiar with a test's subject to learn that subject matter and prepare to take that test. Each chapter breaks down a subject area and concludes with hands-on projects and review questions. A CD-ROM that contains two sample tests is also included.

In addition, you'll probably find any or all of the following materials useful in your quest for Microsoft expertise:

- **Study guides** Numerous publishers offer so-called MCSE study guides of one kind or another.
- **Microsoft Resource Kits** Although not every Microsoft test is the subject of one of these publications (nor of their supplements, two of which are available for Windows NT Server at this writing), all of them include valuable information about Microsoft terminology, products, and technologies. Resource Kits are available from Microsoft Press and are usually must-have resources, not just for test preparation, but for living with these products once you've passed the tests.
- **Classroom training** ATECs, AATPs, MOLI, and unlicensed third-party training companies (such as Wave Technologies, American Research Group, Learning Tree, and Data-Tech) offer classroom training on Microsoft exam topics. These companies aim to help prepare network administrators to understand Microsoft's requirements and pass the tests. Although such training runs upwards of $350 per day in class, most individuals who are lucky enough to partake (including your humble author, who's even taught such courses) find them to be quite worthwhile.
- **Other publications** You'll find plenty of other publications and resources if you take the time to look around on the Web or in your local bookstore; there's no shortage of materials available about Microsoft exams.
- **TechNet** TechNet is a monthly CD subscription available from Microsoft. TechNet includes all the Windows NT BackOffice Resource Kits and their product documentation. In addition, TechNet provides the contents of the Microsoft Knowledge Base and many kinds of software, white papers, training materials, as well as other good stuff. TechNet also contains all service packs, interim release patches, and supplemental driver software released since the last major version for most Microsoft programs and all Microsoft operating systems. A one-year subscription costs $299—worth every penny, if only for the download time it saves.

The previous set of required and recommended materials represents a nonpareil collection of sources and resources for Microsoft exam topics and software.

Need To Know More?

For convenience, I include all the URLs mentioned so far in this chapter, along with pointers to a few other resources worth investigating for information about Microsoft certification, exams, training, and more.

This book's companion CD-ROM contains useful information on Microsoft's certification programs.

www.microsoft.com/train_cert/ This is the ultimate resource for information related to Microsoft certification. Be sure to investigate the buttons on the left-hand side of this home page; the Find An Exam and Certification Choices buttons are particularly useful.

www.microsoft.com/mcp/certstep/mcps.htm This is the home page for Microsoft Certified Professionals. It lists the requirements for and steps necessary to attain this entry-level Microsoft certification status.

www.microsoft.com/mcp/certstep/internet.htm This is the home page for MCP+I information, and lists the requirements for and steps necessary to attain this Internet-focused MCP status.

www.microsoft.com/mcp/certstep/mcp_sb.htm This is the home page for MCP+SB information, and lists the requirements for and steps necessary to attain this Web publishing-focused MCP status.

www.microsoft.com/mcp/certstep/mcse.htm This is the home page for MCSE information, and lists the requirements for and steps necessary to attain this much-vaunted Microsoft level of certification, which is the benchmark for most Microsoft professionals.

www.microsoft.com/mcp/certstep/mcsein.htm This is the home page for MCSE+I information, and lists the requirements for and steps necessary to attain this level of certification, which is the only Microsoft certification more demanding than MCSE.

www.microsoft.com/mcp/certstep/mcsd.htm This is the home page for MCSD information, and lists the requirements for and steps necessary to attain this level of certification, which is the only Microsoft certification aimed specifically at software developers.

www.microsoft.com/office/train_cert/ This is the home page for Microsoft Office User Specialist information, and lists the requirements for and steps necessary to attain the various levels of certification within this category.

www.mous.net/ This is the home page for the MOUS program. It includes information on upcoming tests and events, an electronic newsletter open to all subscribers, and general program information.

www.officecert.com/ This is a third-party MOUS site, operated by QuickStart Technologies, Inc. It features exam information, online study groups, access to domain experts, and more. Worth spending time on, if you're chasing any MOUS credentials.

www.sylvanprometric.com This is the home page for Sylvan Prometric's testing centers, and can provide information about this company's locations, charges, and policies.

www.vue.com/ms This is the home page for Virtual University Enterprises's Microsoft testing area, and can provide information about this company's locations, charges, and policies for such tests.

www.mcpmag.com This URL points to the home page for *Microsoft Certified Professional* magazine, a third-party publication that covers news, products, training materials, study guides, and other information related to Microsoft certification.

www.amazon.com This URL points to Amazon.com, one of the best-known of all the online bookstores.

www.microsoft.com/train_cert/download/downld.htm This URL points to Microsoft's Training And Certification Downloads page, where you can find exam preparation guides, practice tests, and other kinds of self-assessment tools.

www.microsoft.com/technet This URL points to the online version of Microsoft's fabulous TechNet CD library.

www.sunbelt-software.com/mcse.htm This URL points to Sunbelt Software's online resources for MCSE preparation, which includes an informative and active mailing list focused on MCSE issues, plus pointers to all kinds of study and preparation materials.

3

Novell Certification Programs

Terms you'll need to understand:

- ✓ CNA
- ✓ CNE
- ✓ MCNE
- ✓ CIP
- ✓ NetWare product family: NetWare 3, NetWare 4/ IntranetWare, NetWare 5
- ✓ System administrator
- ✓ Network administrator

Techniques you'll need to master:

- ✓ Locating training and certification information on the Novell Web site
- ✓ Obtaining descriptions and objectives for specific Novell exams
- ✓ Locating practice tests to help you prepare for specific Novell exams

Novell has been in the training and certification game long enough to be considered a pioneer, although it may not have the most complex or voluminous set of offerings of all the vendors you'll encounter in this book. Novell's certification program predates Microsoft's by at least three years, and the number of certified professionals—currently estimated at over 400,000 and growing—is the largest of any certification program. In this chapter, you'll examine Novell's various certification options.

Alphabet Soup

To begin, let's review the numerous acronyms that relate to Novell's certification credentials. After that, you'll have a chance to investigate each certification in some detail, including the elements that lead to each one. Along the way, you'll be presented with a series of tables that show how the pieces fit together. Then, you'll learn how to sign up for tests, track certification progress, and prepare for each test.

Here are the acronyms related to Novell certifications, with brief explanations:

- **Certified Novell Administrator (CNA)** Candidates who demonstrate their skills in any of a number of areas of expertise. This certification requires passing one test in any of five tracks (three are specific to NetWare versions and two are specific to GroupWise versions). This is Novell's entry-level certification.
- **Certified Novell Engineer (CNE)** Candidates who demonstrate their skills in installing and managing NetWare networks. This certification is obtained by passing six or seven exams, including five or six (depending on which track you are pursuing) required core exams and a single elective. This is Novell's most sought-after certification.
- **Master CNE (MCNE)** Candidates must first prove their basic expertise by obtaining CNE certification. To obtain an MCNE certification, they must then pass four to six tests in any of seven specialized areas. This is Novell's most elite certification.
- **Certified Internet Professional (CIP)** Candidates who prove their expertise for one or more of a variety of Internet professional roles. These roles include Certified Internet Business Strategist, Certified Web Designer, Certified Web Developer, Certified Intranet Manager, and Certified Internet Architect. To qualify, candidates must pass anywhere from one to five required exams, depending on which role they seek.

All the information in the preceding list, plus some additional details about the exams, is summed up in Table 3.1.

Table 3.1 Novell certifications, exams, and more.

Certification	Required Exams	Elective Exams	Questions	Cost	Time
CNA	1	0	15-74	$95	30-90 min.
CNE	5-6	1	15-74	$95	30-90 min.
MCNE	4-5	0-1	15-74	$95	30-90 min.
CIP	1-5	0	15-74	$95	30-90 min.

The number of questions, the cost, and the time period are for each exam, not for all exams.

Novell uses two different types of tests in its certification exams: program tests and adaptive tests. *Program tests* use traditional, multiple-choice questions, graphical exhibits, and simulations. They follow a regular, predictable sequence of questions, drawn at random, by category, from a database of potential questions. Each test-taker sees the same number of questions, and gets an equal amount of time to finish.

Adaptive tests recognize when test-takers miss a question, and react by asking a simpler question on the same topic, asking gradually more difficult questions on that topic until a test-taker's expertise in the category is established. For this reason, adaptive tests can end in as little as 30 minutes, or can take longer than an hour to complete.

Because the length of an adaptive test is related to the test-taker's familiarity with the subject matter, it's more important to prepare thoroughly for an adaptive test than for a program test. Adaptive behavior also makes it impossible to predict exactly how many questions you'll see on any particular adaptive test, or how long a test will take. That's why Table 3.1 shows broad variation in the number of questions and time required for the various exams it lists. For details on the type and number of questions for any Novell test, please visit **http://education.novell.com/testinfo/testdata.htm**.

In the sections that follow, you'll examine each of Novell's certifications in more detail, and learn a little more about the related exams that you must pass. If you visit the URLs mentioned for each credential, in most cases you'll be able to jump straight to the details related to the required exams (and electives, where applicable).

Although Web locations change over time, they're worth chasing down because Novell's Web site is the final authority on certification information and requirements.

CNA

When it comes to options, CNAs have an awful lot to choose from. But because CNAs provide on-site network and systems administration in a variety of working conditions, this variety makes sense. In general, CNAs are usually responsible for everyday administration and oversight of some installed Novell networking product, be it NetWare 5, IntranetWare or NetWare 4, NetWare 3, GroupWise 5, or GroupWise 4. These specific product responsibilities also match the tracks that prospective CNAs must follow to attain this particular certification.

You many notice throughout this chapter that I use NetWare 4 to refer to the IntranetWare track. This is because Novell uses both names for the same product—namely IntranetWare and NetWare 4.11, but the network operating system software is more commonly referred to as NetWare 4 or 4.x to cover all versions.

Table 3.2 covers the requirements for each CNA category. However, please note that Novell recommends that prospective CNAs meet certain knowledge prerequisites: NetWare CNAs of all stripes should know basic PC and networking concepts and terminology, and be familiar with DOS and Windows; GroupWise CNAs of all stripes should know basic NetWare administration and NetWare Directory Services (NDS).

For a more detailed description of these requirements, visit the CNA home page at **http://education.novell.com/cna/**. For a detailed roadmap of courses, tests, and certifications into which the various CNA tracks feed (and Novell is very good about pointing out how these various tracks can lead to more advanced Novell certifications), download the CNA Progress Chart from the CNA home page.

CNE

Individuals who obtain a CNE are assumed to be qualified to plan, install, configure, and manage the systems and services that fall within the track they are pursuing. Except for a single elective exam, the CNE remains very much a NetWare- or GroupWise-focused certification (only the version of NetWare

Table 3.2 CNA tracks and associated exams.

Exam ID and Title	50-639 NetWare 5 Administration
Track	NetWare 5
Description	Covers basic NetWare 5 planning, installation, configuration, and administration.
Exam ID and Title	50-613 IntranetWare: NetWare 4.11 Administration
Track	NetWare 4
Description	Covers basic NetWare 4.11/IntranetWare planning, installation, configuration, and administration.
Exam ID and Title	50-130 3.1x System Administration
Track	NetWare 3
Description	Covers basic NetWare 3.x (current version is 3.12) planning, installation, configuration, and administration.
Exam ID and Title	50-618 GroupWise 5 Administration
Track	GroupWise 5
Description	Covers GroupWise 5 features, functions, and architecture; planning; installation; administration; user management; libraries; documents; and more.
Exam ID and Title	50-154 GroupWise 4 Administration
Track	GroupWise 4
Description	Covers GroupWise 4 features, functions, and architecture; planning; installation; administration; user management; libraries; documents; and more.

or GroupWise that a CNE specializes in may vary; otherwise, the testing regimen is the same). Table 3.3 lists the exams for those seeking certification in NetWare (version 3, 4, or 5). Table 3.4 lists the exams for those seeking certification in GroupWise (version 4 of 5).

Note: The same tracks apply to the CNE that apply to the CNA.

Please note that the requirements for the NetWare 4 and 5 tracks overlap considerably, but that the NetWare 3 track includes several of its own special elements. Unless you work in an environment that is tied to NetWare 3 for a special reason, you should seek certification on a more recent version of NetWare, preferably NetWare 5.

For more information about the CNE certification, please visit Novell's CNE home page at **http://education.novell.com/cne/**. Pay special attention to the CNE Progress Chart.

Table 3.3 Exams required for NetWare CNE certifications.

Passing any five or six (depending on which track you seek) of the following required exams and any one of the following electives qualifies you as a NetWare CNE. The track's name appears beneath the test number. The Networking Technologies and Service and Support tests are required for all CNEs (the lower-numbered test is more suitable for NetWare 3 or 4 certification; the higher-numbered test is for NetWare 5 certification). Where multiple tests are separated by the keyword **OR**, only one item in that group counts towards certification.

Required Exams

Exam ID and Title	50-147	Networking Technologies		
OR				
Exam ID and Title	50-632	Networking Technologies		
Track	All			
Description	Both tests provide comprehensive coverage of networking design, installation, operations, and troubleshooting, across a broad range of networking technologies and transmission media.			
Exam ID and Title	50-626	Service and Support		
OR				
Exam ID and Title	50-635	Service and Support		
Track	All			
Description	Both tests cover the skills necessary to provide troubleshooting, maintenance, and technical support on NetWare networks. These are widely regarded as two of the most challenging of all the required Novell certification tests.			
Exam ID and Title	50-639	50-613	50-130	NetWare Administration
Track	NetWare 5	NetWare 4	NetWare 3	
Description	These tests cover basic NetWare planning, installation, setup, and administration.			
Exam ID and Title	50-640	50-614	50-131	Advanced NetWare Administration
Track	NetWare 5	NetWare 4	NetWare 3	
Description	These tests cover advanced NetWare installation, configuration, enterprise-level deployment, remote management, and systems integration.			
Exam ID and Title	50-634	NDS Design and Implementation		
OR				
Exam ID and Title	50-601	IntranetWare/NetWare 4.11 Design and Implementation		
Track	NetWare 5 and 4			
Description	Test 50-634 covers advanced use of NetWare Directory Services, including directory planning, design, and deployment; and using multiple directory trees. Test 50-601 covers advanced use of NDS in the context of designing and deploying a complex NetWare 4-based network.			

(continued)

Table 3.3 Exams required for NetWare CNE certifications *(continued)*.

Exam ID and Title	50-615 NetWare 3.x to NetWare 4.11 Update
Track	NetWare 3
Description	Prepares NetWare 3 administrators to upgrade to NetWare 4, or to integrate NetWare 4.x servers with their NetWare 3.x counterparts.
Exam ID and Title	50-617 IntranetWare: NetWare 4.11 Design & Implementation
Track	NetWare 4
Description	Covers basic training on NetWare 4 installation, configuration, and design, for administrators who wish to install and deploy NetWare 4-based networks.
Exam ID and Title	50-132 NetWare 3.1x Installation and Configuration
Track	NetWare 3
Description	Covers NetWare 3.1x installation, planning, and deployment; plus numerous configuration scenarios, aimed at larger, more complex NetWare 3.x environments.
Electives (Any one of these tests fulfills the elective requirement for all three NetWare CNE tracks, except test 50-627, which applies to NetWare 4 only.)	
Exam ID and Title	50-629 Securing Intranets with BorderManager
Description	BorderManager is Novell's sophisticated gateway/firewall/proxy server and Web accelerator product. This exam covers BorderManager's theory of operations, planning, installation, configuration, and maintenance.
Exam ID and Title	50-628 Management Using ManageWise 2.1
Description	ManageWise provides sophisticated system and network management capabilities. This exam covers basic network management principles and practices, remote management and control, integrating with SNMP systems, and more.
Exam ID and Title	50-636 IntranetWare Integrating Windows NT
Description	Covers issues involved in integrating Windows NT servers and workstations into a NetWare environment, where NetWare, NDS, and Windows NT servers and domains are the primary systems.
Exam ID and Title	50-618 GroupWise 5 Administration
Description	Covers GroupWise 5 features, functions, and architecture; planning; installation; administration; user management; libraries; documents; and more.
Exam ID and Title	50-627 Building Intranets with IntranetWare
Description	Covers planning, design, implementation, and theory of operations for constructing and managing in-house intranets. (This elective applies to only the NetWare 4 track.)

Table 3.4 Exams required for GroupWise CNE certifications.

Passing any five of the following required exams and any one of the following electives qualifies you as a GroupWise CNE. The track's name appears beneath the test number. The Networking Technologies and Service and Support tests are required of all CNEs (the lower-numbered test is more suitable for NetWare 3 or 4 certification; the higher-numbered test for NetWare 5 certification). Where multiple tests are separated by the keyword **OR**, only one item in that group counts towards certification.

Required Exams (Pass any five that apply to a specific track.)

Exam ID and Title	50-147	Networking Technologies	
OR			
Exam ID and Title	50-632	Networking Technologies	
Track	All		
Description	Both tests provide comprehensive coverage of networking design, installation, operations, and troubleshooting, across a broad range of networking technologies and transmission media.		
Exam ID and Title	50-626	Service and Support	
OR			
Exam ID and Title	50-635	Service and Support	
Track	All		
Description	Both tests cover the skills necessary to provide troubleshooting, maintenance, and technical support on NetWare networks. These are widely regarded as two of the most challenging of all the required Novell certification tests.		
Exam ID and Title	50-618	50-154	GroupWise Administration
Track	GroupWise 5	GroupWise 4	
Description	Both tests cover GroupWise features, functions, and architecture; planning; installation; administration; user management; libraries; documents; and more.		
Exam ID and Title	50-619	50-604	Advanced GroupWise Administration
Track	GroupWise 5	GroupWise 4	
Description	Both tests cover planning and installing GroupWise applications, document management, workflow, and enterprise-level configuration and management issues.		
Exam ID and Title	50-612	GroupWise 4 Async Gateway and GroupWise Remote	
Track	GroupWise 4		
Description	Covers principles of the GroupWise 4 dial-up gateway, and use of GroupWise 4 remote access capabilities, including planning, design, installation, configuration, and management.		

(continued)

Table 3.4	**Exams required for GroupWise CNE certifications *(continued)*.**	
Exam ID and Title	50-620	GroupWise Net Access and Connectivity
Track	GroupWise 5	
Description	Covers GroupWise gateways and agents; user access methods, protocols, and services; Internet access and gateways; installation; configuration; and management.	
Electives (Any one of these tests fulfills the elective requirement for both GroupWise CNE tracks.)		
Exam ID and Title	50-629	Securing Intranets with BorderManager
Description	Covers theory of BorderManager's operations, planning, installation, configuration, and maintenance.	
Exam ID and Title	50-628	Management Using ManageWise 2.1
Description	Covers basic network management principles and practices, remote management and control, integrating with SNMP systems, RMON, and more.	
Exam ID and Title	50-636	IntranetWare Integrating Windows NT
Description	Covers issues involved in integrating Windows NT servers and workstations into a NetWare environment.	
Exam ID and Title	50-618	GroupWise 5 Administration
Description	Covers GroupWise 5 features, functions, and architecture; planning; installation; administration; user management; libraries; documents; and more.	

MCNE

Novell calls this credential "the industry's leading integration specialists." Given that passing six exams and obtaining a CNE are merely prerequisites to entering the MCNE program, and that four to six additional exams are necessary to make the grade, it may have a point. Suffice it to say that only those with a real appetite for test taking tend to attain this high status.

MCNE exams are broken into three categories, as follows:

- **Core** All MCNEs must take two core exams on internetworking and IntranetWare design and implementation. This is to ensure that all candidates have a solid background in complex, heterogeneous network environments. Some MCNE specialties involve one additional core exam.
- **Target** Each area of specialization involves one or two target tests, to ensure specialists' expertise in their chosen areas.

- **Elective** Most specializations involve one or two elective tests, to make sure that specialists are well-rounded in important Novell or networking technologies.

All relevant tests for the MCNE appear in Table 3.5, broken down by the areas of specialization detailed below. Target exams vary by specialty. The table also includes the number of electives required by specialty, where applicable.

Seven areas of specialization apply to the MCNE, namely:

- **Management** For MCNEs who wish to specialize in network management, operations, and troubleshooting. In addition to the two core exams, this specialty requires one target test and two electives, for a total of five exams. (Abbreviated as Mgmt in Table 3.5.)
- **Connectivity** For MCNEs who wish to specialize in managing communications and access on complex internetworks, usually with WAN as well as LAN connections. In addition to the two core exams, this specialty requires one target exam and two electives, for a total of five exams. (Abbreviated as Conn in Table 3.5.)
- **Messaging** For MCNEs who wish to specialize in email systems or messaging-based applications, usually involving multiple email systems (and gateways) that include GroupWise in their number. In addition to the two core exams, this specialty requires one target exam and two electives, for a total of five exams. (Abbreviated as Msg in Table 3.5.)
- **Internet/Intranet Solutions** For MCNEs who wish to specialize in IP-based networks and services, whether for internal (intranet) use or involving Internet access. In addition to the three core exams, this specialty requires two target exams and one elective, for a total of six exams. (Abbreviated as Int in Table 3.5.)
- **Client/Network Solutions: IntranetWare and AS/400 Integration** For MCNEs who wish to specialize in networks that involve both NetWare and AS/400 systems. In addition to the three core exams, this specialty requires one target exam, for a total of four exams. (Abbreviated as AS/400 in Table 3.5.)
- **Client/Network Solutions: IntranetWare and Unix Integration** For MCNEs who wish to specialize in networks that involve both NetWare and SCO Unix systems. In addition to the three core exams, this specialty requires one target exam, for a total of four exams. (Abbreviated as Unix in Table 3.5.)

- **Client/Network Solutions: IntranetWare and Windows NT Integration** For MCNEs who wish to specialize in networks that involve both NetWare and Windows NT systems. In addition to the three core exams, this specialty requires one target exam and one elective, for a total of five exams. (Abbreviated as WinNT in Table 3.5.)

Please note that if an elective is required as a core exam or a target exam for some specialty, it may not also be counted for elective credit. For further details on the MCNE requirements, please visit the MCNE home page at **http://education.novell.com/mcne/**. Here again, the Master CNE Progress Chart will help to spell out all the requirements and other details.

Table 3.5 Exams required for Master CNE certifications.

These exams are separated by the categories Core, Target, and Elective. Where tracks apply to an exam, the track is named by its abbreviations as it appears in the preceding list. Where an exam applies to all tracks, its category is listed as All. Where any one of several exams may be taken, such exams will be grouped and separated by the keyword **OR** in a single table entry.

Core Exams	
Exam ID and Title	50-611 Fundamentals of Internetworking
Track	All
Description	Covers internetworking protocols, principles, and practices, including the OSI reference model, bridges, routers, gateways, network addressing, security, and so on.
Exam ID and Title	50-601 IntranetWare/NetWare 4.11 Design and Implementation
Track	All
Description	Covers advanced use of NDS and directory structures in the context of designing and deploying a complex NetWare 4-based network.
Exam ID and Title	50-145 NetWare TCP/IP Transport
Track	Int and WinNT
Description	Covers IP protocols, principles, services, addressing, and use on IntranetWare networks.
Exam ID and Title	50-605 NetWare for SAA
Track	AS/400
Description	Covers Novell's IBM host integration package, including protocols, principles, operations, design, installation, configuration, and maintenance.

(continued)

Table 3.5 Exams required for Master CNE certifications *(continued)*.

Exam ID and Title	50-145 NetWare TCP/IP Transport
OR	
Exam ID and Title	90-004 SCO TCP/IP
OR	
Exam ID and Title	90-054 SCO Open Server Network Administration
Track	Unix
Description	Test 50-145 covers IP protocols, principles, services, addressing, and use on IntranetWare networks. Test 90-004 covers IP protocols, principles, services, addressing, and deployment on an SCO Unix server; is an SCO certification test. Test 90-054 covers network administration around SCO's Open Server platform, and a wide range of IP-related topics and issues; is an SCO certification test.
Target Exams	
Exam ID and Title	50-628 Management Using ManageWise 2.1
Track	Mgmt
Description	Covers basic network management principles and practices, remote management and control, integrating with SNMP systems, RMON, and more.
Exam ID and Title	50-629 Securing Intranets with BorderManager
Track	Conn
Description	Covers theory of operations, planning and installation, configuration, and maintenance for Novell's gateway/firewall/proxy server and Web accelerator product.
Exam ID and Title	50-619 GroupWise 5 Advanced Administration
OR	
Exam ID and Title	50-623 GroupWise 4.1 to 5 Differences
Track	Msg
Description	Test 50-619 covers planning and installing GroupWise 5 applications, document management, workflow, and enterprise-level configuration and management issues. Test 50-623 covers upgrade issues for those already certified in GroupWise 4 advanced administration.
Exam ID and Title	50-710 Web Server Management
Track	Int
Description	Covers planning, designing, installing, configuring, and managing a NetWare-based Web server.
Exam ID and Title	50-625 DNS and FTP Server Installation and Configuration
Track	Int
Description	Covers planning, designing, installing, configuring, and managing NetWare-based FTP and DNS servers; and integration with BIND or other external DNS servers, including master-slave setup.

(continued)

Table 3.5 Exams required for Master CNE certifications *(continued)*.

Exam ID and Title	00-051	IBM 1100 IntranetWare and AS/400 Integration
Track	AS/400	
Description	Covers IntranetWare-AS/400 integration issues from the IBM host perspective; is an IBM certification test.	
Exam ID and Title	95-153	SCO Open Server Release 5 ACE for Master CNE
OR		
Exam ID and Title	95-154	SCO UnixWare 2.1 ACE for Master CNE
Track	Unix	
Description	Test 95-153 covers Open Server-to-NetWare integration issues from the SCO Server perspective; is an SCO certification test. Test 95-154 covers UnixWare-to-NetWare integration issues from the UnixWare perspective; is an SCO certification test.	
Exam ID and Title	50-636	IntranetWare Integrating Windows NT
Track	WinNT	
Description	Covers issues involved in integrating Windows NT servers and workstations into a NetWare environment.	
Elective Exams (Each specialty that requires electives can take any of the following. The Management, Connectivity, Messaging, Internet/Intranet Solutions and the IntranetWare and Windows NT Integration require electives.)		
Exam ID and Title	50-606	Fundamentals of Network Management
Exam ID and Title	50-622	Printing in an Integrated NetWare Environment
Exam ID and Title	50-627	Building Intranets with IntranetWare
Exam ID and Title	50-145	NetWare TCP/IP Transport
Exam ID and Title	50-160	NetWare NFS Services: Management, Printing, and File Sharing
Exam ID and Title	50-605	NetWare for SAA
Exam ID and Title	50-628	Network Management Using ManageWise 2.1
Exam ID and Title	50-629	Securing Intranets with BorderManager

CIP

Novell's CIP credential aims to prepare professionals for a variety of Internet-related business roles. Because it's not really part of Novell's network professional certifications per se, I don't cover this credential in great detail. At present, this program is still under construction. Currently, there are only five strictly CIP tests available. The five other tests also apply to other Novell certifications outside the CIP program. This information appears in Table 3.6.

Table 3.6 CIP-related exams.		
Exam ID	**Certification**	**Title**
Certification Key: A=Certified Internet Architect; B=Certified Internet Business Strategist; D=Certified Web Designer; M=Certified Intranet Manager; W=Certified Web Developer		
Exclusive To CIP Certification		
050-700	D, M	Web Authoring and Publishing
050-701	A, B, D, M, W	Internet Business Strategies
050-703	D	Designing an Effective Web Site
050-705	D, M	Advanced Web Authoring
050-710	A, M	Web Server Management
Crossovers From Other Novell Certifications		
050-613	M	IntranetWare/NetWare 4.11 Administration
050-611	A	Fundamentals of Internetworking
050-145	A	NetWare TCP/IP Transport
050-625	A	DNS and FTP Server Installation and Configuration
050-629	A	Securing Intranets with BorderManager

For more information on Novell's CIP program and to keep tabs on late-breaking information about this new certification, please visit the CIP home page at **www.netboss.com**. At present, no progress charts are available. However, you can access descriptions and requirements for each track.

Novell Testing

By now, you've certainly read about a sizable number of Novell tests. You are probably wondering what's involved in signing up for or taking such tests. Nothing could be easier than to explain how this process works!

You may sign up with one of two testing companies that handle testing for Novell certification:

- **Sylvan Authorized Prometric Testing Centers** Sign up through the company's Web site at **www.sylvanprometric.com/clients/Register/sls/aptc/testthrough.htm** (select the Novell hyperlink from this page) or register by phone at 612-820-5706.

- **Virtual University Enterprises (VUE)** Sign up at **www.vue.com/novell/** or register by phone at 612-897-7370.

To sign up for a test, you must have a valid credit card, or contact either company for mailing instructions to send the company a check or money order. You can register for a test only when payment is verified or your check has cleared.

To schedule an exam, call or visit the Web page at least one day in advance. To cancel or reschedule an exam, you must call at least 12 hours before the scheduled test time (or you may be charged, even if you don't show up for the test).

To schedule a test, have the following information:

- Your name, organization, and mailing address.
- Your Novell Education Testing ID and PIN. Inside the United States, the ID is your social security number; citizens of other nations should call ahead to find out what type of identification is needed. The PIN is a number you select when you first sign up to take a Novell certification exam with either Sylvan or VUE. Be sure to write this down somewhere, and have it ready when you sign up.
- The name and number of the exam you wish to take.
- A method of payment.

Once you sign up for a test, you'll be told when and where the test is scheduled. Try to arrive at least 15 minutes early. You must supply two forms of identification, one of which must be a photo ID.

All Novell exams are closed book. In fact, you can't take anything with you into the testing area. You will be given a blank sheet of paper and a pen. I suggest that you immediately write down whatever you've memorized for the test before you begin the test. You will have some time to compose yourself, to record this information, and even to take a sample orientation test before you begin the real thing. I suggest that you take the orientation exam before taking your first real Novell exam. They're all more or less the same in terms of layout, behavior, and controls, so you won't need to do this more than once or twice before it's quite familiar.

As soon as you complete a Novell exam, the software tells you whether you've passed or failed. Even if you fail, I suggest you ask for—and keep—the detailed score report that the test administrator can print for you. This will tell you which areas you need to work on. If you happen to fail, you will have to contact Sylvan or VUE to schedule another test.

Tracking Novell Certification Status

As soon as you pass any of the CNA exams, you'll attain Certified Novell Administrator status. Novell also maintains a Personal Certification Requirements History (PCRH), which indicates the exams you have taken and those you have passed. You can check your PCRH through the secured Novell Power PIN login page at **http://certification.novell.com/pinlogin.htm**.

> *Note: It takes Novell up to seven business days after an exam to update your PCRH.*

In addition to providing access to certification information and test records, Novell operates secured Web sites for CNA, CNE, and CIP candidates. These sites provide access to all types of information aimed at certified users. This information includes special news, software utilities, operating system updates and tools, and opportunities to sign up for beta tests and beta software. You'll find much more than simply access to your certification progress reports. You'll be furnished with details on how to access these sites—which require your Testing ID and PIN to gain access—when you complete any Novell certification exam that qualifies you for a potential certification (thus, aspiring CNEs who finish a test can get access to the site, as well as already certified CNEs).

You can also contact Novell's education operation at 801-222-3382 or send email to **edcustomer@novell.com**.

How To Prepare For Novell Exams

At a minimum, you should use the following materials to prepare for a Novell exam:

- For most exams, Novell offers one or more instructor-led training classes. Novell recommends you attend such training at a Novell Authorized Education Center (NAEC), a Novell Education Academic Partner (NEAP), or an InfiLearning Center. However, other study options are available, including self-study kits, computer-based training, and computer trade books. Novell recommends that you discuss these options with a nearby training center professional.
- Because Novell publishes both course and test objectives, you should also become familiar with these items before taking any test. Course objectives appear in Novell's course catalog at **http://education.novell.com/catalog/**; test objectives are available at **http://education.novell.com/testinfo/objectives/crsindex.htm**.

- Novell publishes The Guide CD-ROM, which you can get from any local testing center at no charge. It contains practice exams with questions very much like those that appear on the actual exams. In fact, it is produced by the same people who write those exams. These are worth taking, if only to get the feel for the real thing.

In addition, you'll probably find any or all of the following materials useful in your search for Novell expertise:

- **Study guides** Numerous publishers offer CNE or CNA study guides of some type. A search at your favorite online bookstore will help in locating these.
- **Other publications** You'll find plenty of other publications and resources if you take the time to look around on the Web or in your local bookstore, but there's no shortage of materials available about Novell.
- **The Network Support Encyclopedia, Professional Edition (NSEPro)** The NSEPro is a monthly CD subscription that includes all types of technical documentation and training materials about Novell products and technologies, plus summaries of technical support issues, and software patches and fixes. A single-user NSEPro license is $495 per year and site licenses cost $995 yearly. However, CNEs can purchase a single-user subscription directly from Novell for $295 per year. To subscribe to the NSEPro, contact an authorized Novell reseller—call 800-828-3362 for a reseller in your area; or call 800-377-4136 or 303-297-2725 to order from Novell directly or to receive your CNE discount.

This set of materials represents a stellar collection of sources and resources for Novell exam topics and software.

Need To Know More?

For convenience, I include the most important URLs mentioned so far in this chapter, along with pointers to a few other resources worth investigating.

http://education.novell.com/certinfo/index.htm Start here to get to the home pages for the CNA, CNE, or MCNE certifications. There, you'll find requirements, progress charts, and more.

www.netboss.com This is the home page for Novell's Certified Internet Professional programs. It lists the requirements for and steps necessary to attain all of the CIP-related certifications.

http://education.novell.com/testinfo/ This is the home page for all Novell certification testing information (except for CIP-only tests). Use this to find objectives, analyze test types, obtain question counts, and more.

http://certification.novell.com/pinlogin.htm This is the Power PIN login page. Once you obtain a Novell Education Testing ID and PIN, visit this page to check your certification status, obtain news about new certification tests and objectives, sign up for beta tests, and so on.

http://support.novell.com This is the home page for Novell Technical Support. It is also an excellent source of technical data, including a meaty and worthwhile set of NetWare 5 white papers.

comp.os.netware.connectivity This is the key technical Usenet newsgroup on Novell technologies and NetWare topics. Other members of this hierarchy are **comp.os.netware.security** (covers NetWare security topics), **comp.os.netware.announce** (covers Novell and third-party NetWare-related announcements), and **comp.os.netware.misc** (covers other NetWare topics that don't fit under the other NetWare newsgroups).

4

Oracle Certification Programs

Terms you'll need to understand:

- √ Oracle Certification Program (OCP)
- √ Database Administrator (DBA) track
- √ Application Developer track
- √ Oracle product family: Oracle7, Oracle8
- √ Instructor-Led Training (ILT)
- √ Media-Based Training (MBT)
- √ Oracle Learning Architecture (OLA)

Techniques you'll need to master:

- √ Locating training and certification information on the Oracle Web site
- √ Obtaining descriptions and objectives for specific Oracle exams
- √ Identifying training and self-study options related to specific Oracle exams

To maintain its position as the market leader in the high-end database business, Oracle recently introduced its Oracle Certified Professional program. Currently focused on Oracle7.3, this program recognizes two tracks for certification: one aimed at database administrators (DBAs) and the other at software developers who build applications that integrate Oracle APIs and services. In this chapter, you'll have a chance to examine Oracle's various certification options, and to understand what each of the two Oracle tracks can prepare you to handle.

Alphabet Soup

To begin with, let's review the numerous acronyms that relate to Oracle's certification credentials. After that, you'll have a chance to investigate each certification in some detail, including the elements that lead to each one. Along the way, you'll be presented with a series of tables that show how the pieces fit together, and learn how to sign up for tests, track certification progress, and so on.

Here are the acronyms related to Oracle certifications, with brief explanations:

- **Oracle Certified Professional (OCP)** This is a catch-all term that identifies anyone who obtains an Oracle certification, either as a DBA or an Oracle software developer. DBA candidates must demonstrate their abilities to install, configure, manage, and maintain Oracle databases; software developer candidates must demonstrate their knowledge of Oracle design and development principles, plus important APIs, report generators, forms-based development tools, and so on.
- **Instructor-Led Training (ILT)** This refers to Oracle Education's comprehensive set of classroom courses for exam preparation and general training. Ultimately, the Oracle exams are derived from classroom experience with students, and Oracle indicates that each ILT class covers all the material necessary to take and pass the related test.
- **Media-Based Training (MBT)** This is Oracle's term for self-paced, computer-based training materials. There's a substantial overlap between MBTs available from Oracle and the various certification exams, but sometimes it's necessary to complete two MBTs to adequately prepare for an exam.
- **Oracle Learning Architecture (OLA)** This is Oracle's term for its Web-based training materials. Although these are largely self-paced, and entirely computer-based, OLA training also includes the opportunity to interact with an instructor via email or online chat. Thus, OLA strikes a balance between the ILT and MBT approaches.

Table 4.1 Oracle certifications, exams, and more.

Certification	Exams	Questions	Cost	Time
OCP, Database Administrator track	4	60-70	$125	60-90 min.
OCP, Application Developer track	5	60-70	$125	60-90 min.

Table 4.1 breaks down the two tracks in terms of number of exams, time and, cost.

The number of questions, the cost, and the time period are for each exam, not for all exams.

Oracle's tests are based on multiple choice questions, most of which relate to usage- or data-based scenarios. Thus, answering questions involves applying your knowledge of Oracle concepts, terminology, tools, and techniques to select among a range of possibilities the best alternative, or requires analyzing different implementation or design approaches to determine which is most effective.

Each test is between 60 and 70 questions. Although the tests are designed to be finished in approximately 60 minutes, test-takers are allowed 90 minutes. It is important to read each question carefully and thoroughly, and to try to anticipate what constitutes "best practices" or "optimal results" when determining how to answer.

In the sections that follow, you'll examine both of the Oracle OCP certifications in more detail, and learn a little more about the exams required to qualify for each. If you visit the URLs mentioned for each credential, in most cases you'll be able to jump straight to the details related to the required exams.

Although Web locations change over time, they're worth chasing down because Oracle's Web site is the most up-to-date source for certification information and requirements.

Please note that Oracle also intends to use its Web site to post recertification information for current OCPs. Oracle requires OCPs to recertify within six months of a new database version's release. Therefore, with Oracle 8 certification approaching, it is probably a good idea to drop in on **http://education.oracle.com** at least monthly.

OCP-DBA Track

This track, formally referred to as the Oracle7.3 Certified Database Administrator track, aims to identify those individuals who understand how to maintain an Oracle database in an enterprise business-computing environment. The certification covers a broad range of skills that include the following:

- Writing routine Oracle queries, analyses, and reports.
- Handling everyday requirements for Oracle database administration.
- Understanding basic Oracle database architectures.
- Planning, creating, maintaining, and migrating Oracle databases.
- Monitoring, tuning, and optimizing Oracle database server performance.
- Handling Oracle database server backup and recovery, including backup and recovery strategies, tools, and techniques.

Obtaining this certification requires passing four tests. These are documented in Table 4.2.

For a more detailed description of these requirements, visit the Oracle Education's home page at **http://education.oracle.com/certification** and click on the Database Administration Track button. From there, you can download files that discuss the DBA track in detail.

Table 4.2 OCP-OBA track required tests.

Test No. and Title	1	Introduction to Oracle: SQL and PL/SQL
Description	Covers basic Oracle concepts and terminology, writing SQL and SQL*Plus queries, using Procedure Builder, working with the Data Manipulation Language (DML) and the Data Definition Language (DDL), and the basics of PL/SQL.	
Test No. and Title	2	Oracle7.3: Database Administration
Description	Covers Oracle database architecture, design, creation, and management of Oracle databases of varying degrees of complexity.	
Test No. and Title	3	Oracle7.3: Backup and Recovery Workshop
Description	Covers database roll-back and roll-forward recovery scenarios, using recommended backup and recovery strategies, applying Oracle backup and recovery tools and techniques.	
Test No. and Title	4	Oracle7.3: Performance Tuning Workshop
Description	Covers Oracle database architecture from a performance standpoint, plus monitoring, analysis, tuning, and optimization of Oracle database structures and underlying system configurations.	

OCP-Application Developer Track

The formal name for this Oracle certification is the Oracle Certified Application Developer Track for Developer/2000 Release 1. Developer/2000 Release 1 is the name of Oracle's Y2K-ready development environment. This certification focuses on preparing database professionals to use Oracle's Developer/2000 Release 1 tools and technologies to build state-of-the-art, database-driven applications. This process requires knowledge of Oracle's reporting and user interface design tools, and understanding of business transactions, SQL, and PL/SQL.

The Oracle Certified Application Developer credential, therefore, requires mastering a broad range of skills, including:

- A thorough understanding of Oracle's query language and procedure building tools, especially SQL and PL/SQL.
- Ability to develop, manage, and use stored procedures and functions, packages, and database triggers.
- Total familiarity with Oracle's forms-based design and editing tool for creation of editors, windows, canvases, views, triggers, and input validation, plus event- and error-handling techniques.
- A thorough knowledge and appreciation of the capabilities of Oracle's Developer/2000 Release 1 reporting tool, including designing, building, and running reports in a variety of simple and complex formats and layouts.

Obtaining this certification requires passing five tests. These are outlined in Table 4.3.

For a more detailed description of these requirements, visit the Oracle Education's home page at **http://education.oracle.com/certification** and click on the Application Developer Track button. From there, you can download files that discuss this track in detail.

Oracle Testing

By now, you've read about eight different Oracle tests. You probably want to know what's involved in signing up for or taking such tests. Nothing could be easier than to explain how this works!

Table 4.3 OCP-Application Developer track required tests.

Test No. and Title	1	Introduction to Oracle: SQL and PL/SQL
Description	Covers basic Oracle concepts and terminology, writing SQL and SQL*Plus queries, using Procedure Builder, working with the Data Manipulation Language (DML) and the Data Definition Language (DDL), and the basics of PL/SQL.	
Test No. and Title	2	Develop PL/SQL Program Units
Description	Covers developing stored procedures; managing procedures, functions, and related dependencies; developing and using packages; and developing database triggers.	
Test No. and Title	3	Developer/2000 Forms 4.5 I
Description	Covers the basics of forms-based applications, including Developer/2000 tool navigation; working with layouts; using client/server PL/SQL; creating forms applications, and modules; handling user input; working with triggers and events; and more.	
Test No. and Title	4	Developer/2000 Forms 4.5 II
Description	Covers advanced forms-based applications, including menu modules, programming function keys, forms-based transactions, managing windows and canvases, working with timers, and managing forms and application characteristics on the fly.	
Test No. and Title	5	Developer/2000 Reports 2.5
Description	Covers using the Developer/2000 report generator for designing, creating, and running reports; building data models; managing report layouts and properties; using triggers; and addressing cross-platform integration issues.	

For all these certification tests, you can sign up with the following testing center:

- **Sylvan Prometric Testing Centers** To register for an OCP exam, call Sylvan at 800-755-EXAM, or visit **http://education.oracle.com/certification/locations.html** for a list of testing locations and phone numbers. You can also call 612-820-5200 outside North America to contact Sylvan's headquarters directly.

To sign up for a test, you must have a valid credit card, or contact Sylvan for mailing instructions to send the company a check or money order. You can register for a test only after payment has been verified or a check has cleared.

To schedule an exam, call at least one day in advance. To cancel or reschedule an exam, you must call at least one day before the scheduled test time (or you may be charged, even if you don't show up for the test). Please note that if you fail an OCP exam, you must wait 30 days before you can register to retake the test.

To schedule a test, have the following information:

- Your name, organization, and mailing address.
- A unique identifier that only you may use. (In the United States, this is your social security number. If you live outside the United States, please call Sylvan to ask what kind of identification you need to provide when you take an OCP exam.)
- The name and number of the exam you wish to take, and the name of the track to which it belongs.
- A method of payment.

Once you sign up for a test, you'll be told when and where the test is scheduled. Try to arrive at least 15 minutes early. You must supply two forms of identification, one of which must be a photo ID.

All Oracle exams are closed book. In fact, you can't take anything with you into the testing area. You will be furnished with a blank sheet of paper and a pen. I suggest that you immediately write down whatever you've memorized for the test before you begin the test. You will have some time to compose yourself, to record this information, and even to take a sample orientation test before you begin the real thing. I suggest that you take the orientation exam before taking your first real Oracle exam; they're all more or less the same in terms of layout, behavior, and controls, so you won't need to do this more than once or twice before it's quite familiar.

As soon as you complete an Oracle exam, the software tells you whether you've passed or failed. It even provides detailed diagnostics information to indicate which areas you should study and which Oracle training materials provide this information. Even if you fail an Oracle exam, I suggest you ask for—and keep—the detailed test results that the test administrator can print for you. This tells you which areas you need to work on. If you happen to fail, you will have to contact Sylvan and schedule another test.

Tracking Oracle Certification Status

As soon as you pass the sequence of exams for either Oracle certification track, you'll attain OCP status. Sylvan currently keeps track of this status information, so you'll need to contact Sylvan by phone to request such information if you ever need it.

Note: It takes Sylvan up to 10 business days after an exam to update your certification status.

Also, it takes about 30 days for Sylvan to mail your OCP certificate once you pass all the necessary tests (be sure to keep this certificate in a safe place; replacements cost $10 each). You should also keep copies of your test results in case there is a question of whether you passed a certain test or tests. You can also contact Oracle Education at 800-633-0575 (inside North America) or at 650-506-7000 with questions about status.

How To Prepare For Oracle Exams

At a minimum, you should use the following materials to prepare for an Oracle certification exam:

- For most exams, Oracle offers corresponding ILT classes. The company recommends that you attend such training through an Oracle-authorized education outlet, which you can arrange through Oracle Education at 800-633-0575 (outside North America, please call 650-506-7000 and ask for Oracle Education). For all OCP topics, however, MBTs and OLAs are also available; call Oracle Education for the details. Oracle also operates an OCP Help Desk, which you can use to register for future exams. Call it at 888-316-7225.
- Because Oracle publishes both course and test outlines, it also recommends that you familiarize yourself with these items prior to taking any test. Course objectives and test outlines appear in Oracle's program guides for both of its certification tracks. You can download them from **http://education.oracle.com/certification/cert_guide.html**.
- Oracle offers assessment tests for aspiring OCPs. If you visit the Sample Tests Web page at **http://education.oracle.com/education/cgi-bin/certform.cgi** and fill out the form, you can download practice exams. Because these exams contain questions much like those that appear on the real tests, they are worth taking.

In addition, you'll probably find any or all of the following materials useful in your search for Oracle expertise:

- **Study guides** Numerous publishers offer Oracle DBA and Application Developer study guides of some type. A search at your favorite online bookstore will help in locating these.

- **Other publications** You'll find plenty of other publications and resources if you take the time to look around on the Web or in your local bookstore, but there's no shortage of materials available about Oracle database technology.

The preceding set of materials represents a manageable collection of sources and resources for OCP exam topics and related information.

Need To Know More?

For convenience, I include the most important URLs mentioned so far in this chapter, along with pointers to a few other resources worth investigating for information about Oracle certification, exams, training, and more.

http://education.oracle.com/certification/ This is the home page for OCP information, and includes ready access to program guides for both OCP tracks, test-taking information, and self-assessment tests. This should be your first stop in any search for OCP information.

Oracle also provides an overall OCP program guide and program guides for the DBA and Application Developer tracks. All of these documents are worth downloading and reading, and provide some of the most detailed and cogent information about the exams, including course and exam outlines.

www.amazon.com A quick search using "Oracle" calls up a number of Oracle-specific books. These should offer some insight into the exam topics, questions, and the exam writers' mindsets.

listserv@ccvm.sunysb.edusend If you send a message that reads "SUBSCRIBE ORACLE-L *<your email address>*" to this address, it will sign you up for one of the best all-around Oracle mailing lists. Another alternative is listserv@kbs.net; send a message that reads "NET SUBSCRIBE ORACLE-L".

The following Usenet newsgroups cover Oracle's products and technologies:

- **comp.databases.oracle** Oracle SQL database products
- **comp.databases.oracle.marketplace** Oracle-related jobs, and so on
- **comp.databases.oracle.server** Oracle database and server administration
- **comp.databases.oracle.tools** Oracle software tools and applications

5

Cisco Career Certification Programs

Terms you'll need to understand:

- √ Cisco Certified Network Associate (CCNA)
- √ Cisco Certified Network Professional (CCNP)
- √ Cisco Certified Internetwork Expert (CCIE)
- √ Cisco Certified Design Associate (CCDA)
- √ Cisco Certified Design Professional (CCDP)
- √ Certification ladder
- √ Laboratory evaluation

Techniques you'll need to master:

- √ Locating training and certification information on the Cisco Web site
- √ Understanding Cisco's individual certifications and its certification ladder
- √ Obtaining descriptions and objectives for specific Cisco exams
- √ Identifying training and self-study options related to specific Cisco exams

To maintain its position as the market leader in the routing, switching, and connectivity business, Cisco offers its Cisco Career Certification programs, chief among them the Cisco Certified Internetwork Expert (CCIE) credential. It also offers two additional levels of networking credentials and two design credentials, for a total of five separate certifications. All the Cisco certifications require advanced skills in supporting a variety of networking topologies and technologies.

Cisco organizes its entire certification program around three specialty tracks: Routing and Switching, ISP Dial, and WAN Switching. The Routing and Switching specialty aims to identify those individuals who understand how to manage a complex internetworked environment that incorporates high-end routers and switches. The ISP Dial specialty aims to identify those individuals who understand how to manage a typical internetworked Internet Service Provider (ISP) environment that incorporates routers and WAN links, and is focused on managing short-haul communications, modem banks, and related issues. The WAN Switching specialty aims to identify those individuals who understand how to manage a complex internetworked environment that incorporates high-end routers and WAN links, and is focused on managing long-haul communications, leased lines, and telephony-related issues.

Individuals typically obtain certification in only one of the three areas, no matter which of the five certifications they pursue. In this chapter, you'll have a chance to examine Cisco's various certification credentials, and to understand what each of the three Cisco certification specialties can prepare you to handle.

Alphabet Soup

To begin with, let's review Cisco's certification programs. After that, you'll have a chance to investigate each of the three tracks, and each individual certification, in some detail, including the elements that lead to each one. Along the way, you'll be presented with a table that shows how the pieces fit together, and learn how to sign up for tests, track certification progress, and so on.

At present, there are five acronyms related to Cisco certification. They describe three certifications related to networks or internetworks, and two certifications related to design:

- **Cisco Certified Network Associate (CCNA)** This is the entry-level operational certification and is aimed at individuals who must manage simple routed LANs or WANs, small ISPs, or smaller switched LAN or LANE environments. Applicants must pass one exam (640-407 for the ISP Dial and Routing and Switching tracks, and 640-410 for the WAN Switching track) to obtain this certification.

- **Cisco Certified Network Professional (CCNP)** This is the middle-tier operational certification, aimed at individuals who must install, configure, operate, and troubleshoot complex routed LANs, routed WANs, switched LAN networks, or Dial Access Services. Applicants must first obtain a CCNA, and then take either two or four additional exams, depending on which test option they select.
- **Cisco Certified Internetwork Expert (CCIE)** This is the top-tier operational certification, aimed at individuals who have advanced technical skills and knowledge, and who must know how to configure networks for optimum performance. They must also understand how to maintain complex, far-flung, multivendor networks. Applicants must pass only two tests for this certification: a written exam and a laboratory evaluation. No prior certification from Cisco is required to obtain a CCIE, but many individuals elect to obtain a CCNA and/or a CCNP before attempting the CCIE.
- **Cisco Certified Design Associate (CCDA)** This is the entry-level design credential; it requires individuals to be able to design and deploy simple routed and switched networks, as well as configure, operate, and maintain such networks. To obtain this certification, applicants must pass one exam (9E0-004). This certification is not available for the WAN Switching specialty.
- **Cisco Certified Design Professional (CCDP)** This is the middle-tier design credential, which requires individuals to be able to design and deploy complex routed LANs and WANs, plus switched LANs and LANE environments. Individuals must also be able to configure, operate, and maintain such networks and connections. To obtain this certification, applicants must typically obtain both a CCNA and CCDA certification (but because there is no CCNA or CCDA certification for the WAN Switching track, only the CCNP is a necessary prerequisite for CCDA candidates in that track), and then pass either two or four more exams, depending on which exam option they elect (I will provide the exam numbers later in this chapter).

This combination of programs creates a "certification ladder," as shown in Figure 5.1.

Thus, a CCNA can lead to either an entry-level design credential (CCDA) or to a middle-tier network credential (CCNP) if the candidate takes a few additional tests. Likewise, both the CCNA and the CCDA lead to the CCDP. And, although the CCIE comes with no prerequisites elsewhere in Cisco's ladder, it is clearly the ultimate Cisco certification, and is where many individuals who obtain other Cisco certifications aim their highest aspirations.

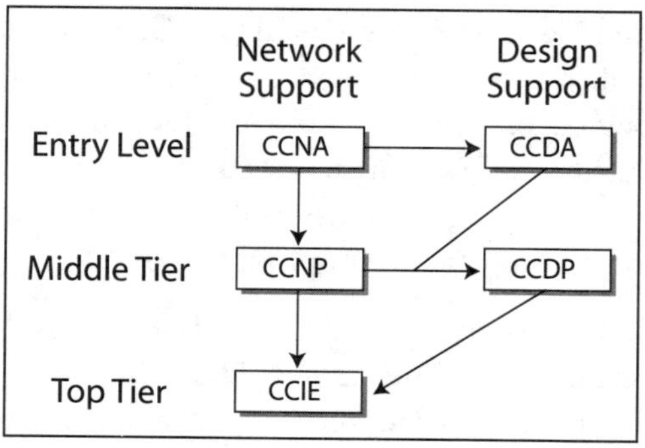

Figure 5.1 The Cisco certification ladder.

All the exam-related information that applies to obtaining a Cisco certification, plus some additional details about the exams, is summed up in Table 5.1. Please note that information about the number of questions, the cost, and the time period is for each exam, not for all exams.

Details about specific test numbers for the CCNP, CCIE, and CCDP certifications are covered later in this chapter. The CCNP and CCDP certifications offer two options; to the left of the slash is the information about Test Option 1 and to the right is the information about Test Option 2. For the CCIE certification, the entries for questions, cost, and time reflect separate entries for the written test (these appear to the left of the slash) and for the laboratory evaluation (these appear to the right of the slash).

Table 5.1 Cisco certifications, exams, and more.

Certification	Prerequisites	Required Exams	Questions	Cost	Time
CCNA	None	1	60	$100	90 min.
CCNP	CCNA	2/4	64-132	$100-$200	90-165 min.
CCIE	None	2	100-123/ varies	$200/ $1,000	120 min./ 2 days
CCDA	CCNA	1	100	$100	180 min.
CCDP*	CCNA, CCDA	2/4	64-132	$100-$200	90-165 min.

* Note that this only applies for the ISP Dial and Routing and Switching specialties. For the WAN CCDP certification, you only need to have a CCNP and pass one exam.

CCNA And CCDA

The CCNA and CCDA certifications require that you pass only one test. Except for these brief descriptions, I provide no more information about these certifications:

- **CCNA exam (640-407)** Titled the Cisco Certified Network Associate test, this test applies to individuals in the Switching and Routing and ISP Dial tracks. This exam covers basic networking knowledge, router configuration and operations, IP addressing and subnets, and more. For a detailed list of objectives, visit **http://www.cisco.com/warp/public/10/wwtraining/certprog/wan/programs/ccna.html.**
- **CCNA exam (640-410)** Titled the Cisco Certified Network Associate WAN Switching exam, this exam covers basic WAN knowledge, LAN/WAN router configuration and operations, IP addressing and subnets, WAN security, and more. For a detailed list of objectives, visit **www.cisco.com/warp/public/10/wwtraining/certprog/lan/programs/CCNA_Test_obj.pdf.**
- **CCDA exam (9E0-004)** Titled the Cisco Design Specialist test, this exam carries the contents of the CCNA test from the operational realm into the design realm. Thus, although it covers the same range of topics and objectives as the CCNA test, its focus is on how to design and implement the technologies, tools, and hardware involved, rather than on using them (as in the CCNA test).

  ***Note:** As of this writing, there is no CCDA certification for the WAN Switching track.*

For a complete listing of all current Cisco certification tests, please visit **www.cisco.com/warp/public/10/wwtraining/certprog/lan/programs/examlist.pdf.**

CCNP

Although the subject matter for the three tracks varies, the exams across these tracks remain the same. For all three specialty tracks, you have two or three exam sequence options, discussed next. Please note that the Foundations exam explained in Step 2 of Test Option 1 for the Routing and Switching and ISP Dial tracks is actually the same as the three tests in Step 2 of Test Option 2 for those same tracks; the Foundations exam has just been separated into its three counterparts in Test Option 2. At $300, Test Option 1 is a better deal than

Test Option 2, at $400, for individuals pursuing either the Routing and Switching or ISP Dial tracks.

As usual, the WAN Switching track differs considerably. As I'm writing this, in fact, the whole WAN Switching track for CCNP is under revision and a great deal of information is not yet available, which is why I do not cover this track in detail. For the latest details, please visit the Web page at **www.cisco.com/warp/public/10/wwtraining/certprog/wan/programs/ccnp.html**.

Test Option 1 For Routing And Switching And ISP Dial Tracks

- **Step 1: CCNA Certification** The CCNA certification is a prerequisite for CCNP certification and must be completed for both test options.
- **Step 2: Foundation Routing and Switching (FRS) Exam (640-409)** This test covers fundamentals and operation of routers and switches, and related Cisco products, in excruciating detail. This exam includes 132 questions, can last as long as 165 minutes, and is the only Cisco test that costs $200 (all others cost $100). For a complete list of objectives, consult **www.cisco.com/warp/public/10/wwtraining/certprog/lan/programs/FRS_Test_Obj.pdf**.
- **Step 3: Cisco Internetwork Troubleshooting (CIT) Exam (640-406)** This test covers the fundamentals and basic principles of network troubleshooting, and of troubleshooting related Cisco products. This exam includes 69 questions, can last as long as 60 minutes, and costs $100. For more information about this test, please consult the information about Cisco's CIT class on its Web site (accessible through any of the CCNP certification pages at **www.cisco.com/warp/public/10/wwtraining/certprog/index.html**).

Test Option 2 For Routing And Switching And ISP Dial Tracks

- **Step 1: CCNA Certification** The CCNA certification is a prerequisite for CCNP certification and must be completed for both test options.
- **Step 2** Applicants must complete three tests, as follows:
  - **Advanced Cisco Router Configuration (ACRC) Exam (640-403)** This exam covers all the details involved in installing and configuring Cisco routers, across the entire product family. This exam includes 72 questions, can take as long as 90 minutes, and costs $100.

- **Cisco LAN Switch Configuration (CLSC) Exam (640-404)** This exam covers installing, configuring, and troubleshooting Cisco's LAN switches. It includes 70 questions, can take as long as 60 minutes, and costs $100.
- **Configuring, Monitoring, and Troubleshooting Dialup Services (CMTD) Exam (640-405)** This exam covers dialup service issues from installation and configuration, through operation and troubleshooting. This exam includes 64 questions, can take as long as 90 minutes, and costs $100.

- **Step 3: Cisco Internetwork Troubleshooting (CIT) Exam (640-406)** This test covers the fundamentals and basic principles of network troubleshooting, and of troubleshooting related Cisco products. This exam includes 69 questions, can last as long as 60 minutes, and costs $100. For more information about this test, please consult the information about Cisco's CIT class on its Web site (accessible through any of the CCNP certification pages at **www.cisco.com/warp/public/10/wwtraining/certprog/index.html**).

CCDP

The CCDP represents a logical step up from the CCNA and CCDA in the Cisco certification ladder, moving over from the CCNA and up from the CCDA; perhaps that's why both of these credentials are normally prerequisites to obtaining CCDP certification. Please note that the Foundations exam explained in Step 3 of Test Option 1 is actually the same as the three tests in Step 3 of Test Option 2; the Foundations exam has just been separated into its three counterparts in Test Option 2. At $300, Test Option 1 is a better deal than Test Option 2, at $400. You will also note that the CCNP and CCDP certifications sometimes overlap in that both require the Foundations exam or its three separate counterparts (as with other elements of the Cisco certification program, this is not true for the WAN Switching track, but does apply to the Switching and Routing and ISP Dial tracks).

Test Option 1 For Routing And Switching And ISP Dial Tracks

- **Step 1: CCNA Certification** The CCNA certification is a prerequisite for CCDP certification and must be completed for both test options.
- **Step 2: CCDA Certification** The CCDA certification is another prerequisite for CCDP certification and must be completed for both test options.

- **Step 3: Foundation Routing and Switching (FRS) Exam (640-409)** This test covers fundamentals and operation of routers and switches, and related Cisco products, in excruciating detail. This exam includes 132 questions, can last as long as 165 minutes, and is the only Cisco test that costs $200 (all others cost $100). For a complete list of objectives, consult **www.cisco.com/warp/public/10/wwtraining/certprog/lan/programs/FRS_Test_Obj.pdf**.
- **Step 4: Cisco Internetwork Design (CID) 3.0 Student Level Exam (640-025)** The exam is based on the Cisco CID class, which covers internetwork troubleshooting in depth, including Cisco hardware, software diagnostics, and monitoring and measurement tools. It includes 100 questions, can last as long as 120 minutes, and costs $100.

Test Option 2 For Routing And Switching And ISP Dial Tracks

- **Step 1: CCNA Certification** The CCNA certification is a prerequisite for CCNP certification and must be completed for both test options.
- **Step 2: CCDA Certification** The CCDA certification is another prerequisite for CCDP certification and must be completed for both test options.
- **Step 3** Applicants must complete three tests, as follows:
  - **Advanced Cisco Router Configuration (ACRC) Exam (640-403)** This test covers all the details involved in installing and configuring Cisco routers, across the entire product family. It includes 72 questions, can take as long as 90 minutes, and costs $100.
  - **Cisco LAN Switch Configuration (CLSC) Exam (640-404)** This exam covers installing, configuring, and troubleshooting Cisco LAN switches. It includes 70 questions, can take as long as 60 minutes, and costs $100.
  - **Configuring, Monitoring, and Troubleshooting Dialup Services (CMTD) Exam (640-405)** This exam covers dialup service issues from installation and configuration, through operation and troubleshooting. It includes 64 questions, can take as long as 90 minutes, and costs $100.
- **Step 4: Cisco Internetwork Design (CID) 3.0 Student Level Exam (640-025)** This exam is based on the Cisco CID class, which covers internetwork troubleshooting in depth, including Cisco hardware,

software diagnostics, and monitoring and measurement tools. It includes 100 questions, can last as long as 120 minutes, and costs $100.

CCIE

Although Cisco requires that candidates pass only two tests to obtain a CCIE, no matter what track is involved, they're both formidable. In the sections that follow, I'll discuss each of these important prices to the CCIE puzzle.

The CCIE Qualification Exam

The written exam, called the CCIE Qualification Exam, is one of the longer exams offered by Sylvan, who administers the written exam (see the "Signing Up For The Written Exams" section later in this chapter). However, only three other elements of the Cisco testing regimen exceed its length. No matter what track you might follow, the CCIE Qualification Exam is regarded as a challenging test of one's Cisco product knowledge, as well as one's general knowledge of networking and communications.

The written exam consists of 100 multiple-choice questions or more; many of which are scenario-based. The nature of a typical exam question makes it important to read it carefully and thoroughly, and to try to anticipate what constitutes "best practices" or "optimal results" when selecting an answer. The exam is graded pass/fail, and candidates are informed whether they passed or not at its conclusion. You must pass the CCIE Qualification Exam before you can sign up for the second exam.

The Laboratory Evaluation

None of the other vendor programs offers an exam anything like Cisco's second CCIE test: a two-day laboratory evaluation, offered at a limited number of testing labs worldwide, for $1,000. Here, would-be CCIEs are subjected to a variety of simulated situations that test their hands-on abilities and diagnostic skills. They must do the following:

- Implement a network or a communications environment from scratch
- Reconfigure existing environments
- Troubleshoot multiple environments that have been deliberately misconnected, misconfigured, or otherwise messed with

I'm told that each of this test's two days can sometimes be quite long, and that the situations posed require extensive product knowledge, manual dexterity, and serious networking skills, along with an ability to think and act quickly and decisively.

In fact, Cisco's tests are so demanding that Cisco publishes the following list of prerequisites to prospective CCIE candidates, no matter what track they may seek to follow:

- A minimum of two years of internetwork administration, if not more
- Hands-on experience with internetwork installation and troubleshooting
- Strong knowledge of Cisco products, including related product and service documentation
- Extensive hands-on experience with Cisco products in a production environment

None of the other vendors is quite so forthcoming about informing prospective candidates that experience is not only advisable, but also necessary. But then, none of the other vendors has such demanding certification requirements either.

Cisco Testing

By now, you've read about many different Cisco tests. You probably want to know what's involved in signing up for or taking such tests. Nothing could be easier than to explain how this works, as long as you remember that one process is required to sign up for the written tests and another to sign up for the CCIE laboratory evaluation.

Signing Up For The Written Exams

You can take the written exams only through Sylvan. To register for a written Cisco certification exam, call Sylvan at 800-204-3926; outside North America, contact Sylvan's headquarters directly at 612-820-5200. You can also check the Cisco Web site at **www.cisco.com/warp/public/625/ccie/qualification.html** for a list of contact numbers for use outside North America.

To sign up for a test, you must possess a valid credit card, or contact Sylvan for mailing instructions to send the company a check or money order. You will be able to register for a test only after payment is verified or your check has cleared.

To schedule an exam, call at least one day in advance. To cancel or reschedule an exam, you must call at least one day before the scheduled test time (or you may be charged, even if you don't show up for the test).

When you want to schedule a test, please have the following information ready:

- Your name, organization, and mailing address.
- A unique identifier that only you may use. (In the United States, this is your social security number. If you live outside the United States, call

Sylvan to ask what kind of identification you need to provide when you take a Cisco exam.)

- The name and number of the exam you wish to take.
- A method of payment.

Once you sign up for a test, you'll be informed as to when and where the test is scheduled. Try to arrive at least 15 minutes early. You must supply two forms of identification to be admitted into the testing room, one of which must be a picture ID.

All Cisco written exams are closed book. In fact, you can't take anything with you into the testing area; you will be furnished with a blank sheet of paper and a pen. I suggest that you immediately write down whatever you've memorized for the test before you start the test. You will have some time to compose yourself, to record this information, and even to take a sample orientation test before you begin the real thing. I suggest that you take the orientation exam; it'll help you get more comfortable when you take the real Cisco test.

As soon as you complete your exam, the software tells you whether you've passed or failed. It also provides a report about your performance on various areas. Even if you fail the exam, I suggest you ask for—and keep—the detailed test results that the test administrator can print for you. You can use these results to help you prepare to retake a test, if necessary. If you are pursuing CCIE certification, you will also need to send Cisco the results to verify that you've passed the written exam so that you may sign up for the laboratory exam. Alas, if you do need to retake an exam, you'll have to schedule another test, and pay the fee again.

Tracking certification progress for Cisco exams also involves following one of two paths: To check on any written exam, you can call Sylvan to obtain a transcript of your test record (a fee of $10 will be charged for each such request). To check on your test record for the lab exam, you'll have to call the test center where you took that exam to obtain the results (described more fully in the section that follows next).

Signing Up For The CCIE Laboratory Evaluation

The laboratory evaluations must be scheduled through and taken at Cisco's facilities. To begin with, full payment must be received at least 21 days before the laboratory evaluation date (28 days for purchase orders in Europe); otherwise, prospective candidates will be dropped. Typically, this means signing up at least two months in advance, if not sooner. Cancellations must be received at least 21 days prior to the test (28 days in Europe); otherwise, the payment is forfeited. Finally, if you fail a laboratory evaluation, you must wait at least 30 days before making another attempt.

To sign up for either the Routing and Switching or WAN Switching CCIE laboratory evaluations, you must call one of the CCIE departments at Cisco at the testing center you want to take the test. At corporate headquarters in San Jose, CA that number is 800-553-6387 or 408-526-8063; you can also fax Cisco at 408-527-8588 or send an email to **ccie_usa@cisco.com**. For testing locations and contact information, please consult the Web page at **www.cisco.com/warp/public/625/ccie/lab.html**.

The ISP Dial exam may only be taken in Halifax, Nova Scotia, Canada. To sign up for this test, call Cisco at 800-553-6387 or 902-492-8811; you can also fax Cisco at 902-492-3926 or send an email to **ccie_ucsa@cisco.com**.

Before you can schedule any laboratory evaluation, the CCIE administrator at Cisco must receive proof that you've passed the CCIE Qualification Exam. The usual approach is to fax the printout of your exam results to the CCIE laboratory evaluation location of your choice, or to 902-492-3926 for the ISP Dial test. Please be sure to include your name, address, phone, and fax number, so your requests can be answered.

How To Prepare For Cisco Exams

At a minimum, you should use the following study materials to prepare for Cisco certification:

- For most exams, Cisco offers several corresponding classes. The company recommends that you attend such training through a Cisco Training Partner. You can arrange to do so through your local Cisco account representative, or through your nearest Cisco location. In North America, call 800-553-6387; outside North America, call 408-526-4000 and ask to speak to an education representative. You can also obtain a complete list of contact numbers from the Web page at **www.cisco.com/warp/public/625/ccie/ccie4_pl.htm**.
- Because Cisco publishes both course and test outlines and objectives, it also recommends that you familiarize yourself thoroughly with these items prior to taking any test. Course objectives and test outlines are accessible through the various certification pages mentioned earlier in this chapter.
- Each of Cisco's certification pages includes pointers to practice tests. Because these exams contain questions like those found on real exams, they're worth taking.

In addition, you'll probably find any or all of the following materials useful in your search for Cisco expertise:

- **Study guides** Most large computer-book publishers offer Cisco certification-related titles.
- **Other publications** You'll find plenty of other publications and resources if you take the time to look around on the Web or in your local bookstore, but there's no shortage of materials available about Cisco technologies and Cisco certification preparation. A quick visit to Amazon.com turned up 23 titles using "Cisco" as a search term.

This set of materials represents a formidable collection of sources and resources for Cisco exam topics and related information.

Need To Know More?

For convenience, I include the most important URLs mentioned so far in this chapter, along with pointers to a few other resources worth investigating for information about Cisco certification, exams, training, and more.

www.cisco.com/warp/public/10/wwtraining/certprog/index.html/ This is the home page for all Cisco certification information, and includes ready access to guides for all certification programs, certification tracks, test-taking information, and self-assessment tests. This should be your first stop in any search for Cisco certification information.

www.cisco.com/warp/public/625/ccie/ This is the home page for CCIE information, and includes ready access to guides on all CCIE tracks, test-taking information, and self-assessment tests. This should be your first stop in any search for CCIE information.

www.cisco.com/warp/public/625/ccie/routing.html This site points to online details on Routing and Switching CCIE certification. It also includes pointers to sample questions for practice.

www.cisco.com/warp/public/625/ccie/cciwa_ds.html This site points to online details on the WAN Switching CCIE certification. It also includes pointers to sample questions for practice.

http://www.cisco.com/warp/public/625/ccie/isp_dial.html This site points to online details on the ISP Dial CCIE certification. This page also includes pointers to sample questions for practice.

www.amazon.com During a quick visit to Amazon.com, I found 23 books on Cisco topics. Many of these should offer some insight into exam topics, questions, and the like.

www.ccieprep.com The site's name says it all—it's entirely devoted to helping its users take and pass the CCIE exams. Although there is a fee required to subscribe to this site, it's a great place to go looking for information outside the Cisco umbrella, and includes great information about laboratory evaluation scenarios.

6

CompTIA A+ Certification

Terms you'll need to understand:

- √ A+
- √ Network+
- √ Certified Document Imaging Architech (CDIA)
- √ Computing Technology Industry Association (CompTIA)

Techniques you'll need to master:

- √ Locating training and certification information on the CompTIA Web site
- √ Obtaining descriptions and objectives for A+ exams
- √ Identifying training and self-study options related to A+ exams

The story behind the A+ exam is a bit different from what you've read about so far. There is no single vendor standing behind A+; rather, this exam results from the efforts of the Computing Technology Industry Association (CompTIA), an industry trade association that currently involves more than 7,500 members around the world.

As a result, a committee composed of numerous vendors and organizations defines the A+ certification, as opposed to one vendor deciding how best to position, support, and promote its products. Thus, the A+ exam is a test designed to certify that individuals are competent PC technicians, and that their knowledge covers hardware and software products, principles, and technologies from many vendors. The official designation for this test's orientation is, in fact, "vendor-neutral."

> CompTIA is working on another exam, called Network+, that aims to provide vendor-neutral network certification some time early in 1999. Because this test has not yet been released, you will only have a chance to read a brief description of its proposed contents, availability, and objectives. Stay tuned to CompTIA's Web site at **www.comptia.org** for more details about release dates, prices, and availability.

A+ Details

To begin with, let's review the A+ certification program. After that, you'll have a chance to review each of the two tests you must pass to obtain this credential, including an overview, objectives, and so on. Along the way, you'll be presented with a table that shows how the pieces fit together. You'll also learn how to sign up for the tests, track progress toward A+ certification, and keep tabs on late-breaking news from CompTIA.

At present, only one certification is relevant to the objectives of this book—namely, the A+ certification for PC technicians (for once, A+ doesn't really stand for anything, either). CompTIA offers another certification—the Certified Imaging Document Architech (CDIA)—but it doesn't attract a sufficiently large audience to merit coverage in this book. (For more information, the home page for this certification is: **www.comptia.org/ct_cdia/**.)

The A+ certification is intended to identify individuals as qualified entry-level PC technicians. The official definition of A+ (taken from CompTIA's page at **www.comptia.org/t_aplus/**) reads as follows: "Earning A+ certification means that the individual possesses the knowledge, skills, and customer relations skills necessary for a successful entry-level (six months' experience) computer service technician…".

To be a bit more specific, obtaining an A+ certification requires passing two tests:

- A Core exam, which stresses basic PC hardware, networking interfaces and connections, and customer support skills.
- A DOS/Windows exam, which stresses basic DOS and Windows architectures, installation, configuration, maintenance, and networking skills.

Thus, someone who obtains an A+ certification is expected to have a broad and thorough understanding of basic PC hardware and software, including assembly or installation, setup and configuration, management, troubleshooting, and end-user support issues.

All the exam-related information that relates to obtaining the A+ certification is summed up in Table 6.1, which lists the number of questions, the cost, and the time period for each of the two current A+ exams.

The lower costs apply only to companies that are members of CompTIA. If your company is not a CompTIA member, you must pay the higher price. Please also note that you get a discount if you sign up and pay for both tests at the same time (you don't need to take both tests on the same day, only within 90 days of each other).

In the sections that follow, you'll examine both of the A+ certification tests in more detail, and learn a little more about what's on each of those exams. If you visit the URLs mentioned for each exam, in most cases you'll be able to jump straight to the nitty-gritty details about each.

> Although Web locations change over time, they're worth chasing down, because CompTIA's Web site is the most up-to-date source for A+ certification information and requirements. The home page for A+ information is **www.comptia.org/ct_aplus/**. From here, you can find all the details you might want. Please note also that the banner advertisements that run on this site provide links to companies that offer A+ training, preparation materials, practice tests, and more.

Table 6.1 A+ exams.

Certification	Questions	Cost (Single Test)	Cost (Both Tests)	Time
Core	69	\$85 or \$120	\$140 or \$215	60 min.
DOS/Windows	70	\$85 or \$120	\$140 or \$215	75 min.

A+ Core Exam

This exam covers basic PC hardware knowledge and related skills. It aims to identify those individuals who understand how to assemble, configure, and maintain PCs, and who can also handle basic networking hardware and end-user support issues. This test was developed from an industry-wide task force of PC technicians. Over 5,000 already-certified A+ technicians were also surveyed on the questions to verify their accuracy. The topics covered in this 69-question exam may be broken down as follows:

- Thirty percent of the questions on the exam relate to installing, configuring, and upgrading PCs.
- Twenty percent of the questions relate to diagnosing problems and troubleshooting PCs.
- Ten percent relate to PC safety and preventive maintenance issues.
- Ten percent of the questions cover issues related to PC motherboards; CPUs; and memory installation, configuration, and upgrades.
- Ten percent of the questions cover issues related to PC-based printers, including cabling, drivers and installation, operation, maintenance, and troubleshooting.
- Five percent of the questions deal with portable PC systems, such as notebooks and laptop computers.
- Five percent of the questions deal with basic networking, primarily network interfaces, connectors, and cabling issues, in keeping with the hardware focus of this test.
- Ten percent of the questions cover customer satisfaction issues, and touch on basic end-user communications, support, and relationship skills.

For more information about test topics and sample questions from each category of questions, please visit the Core exam objectives page at **www.comptia.org/ct_aplus/html/body_core_obj.html**. The exam code for the Core exam is 220-101.

DOS/Windows Exam

This exam covers PC operating system knowledge, and deals with DOS versions 6 and 7, Windows 3.x, and Windows 95. It aims to identify those individuals who understand how to install, configure, maintain, and troubleshoot these operating systems, and who can handle basic networking software and related configuration issues. This test was developed in the same fashion as the Core exam. The topics covered in this 70-question exam include the following:

- Thirty percent of the questions relate to the function, structure, and operation of these operating systems, plus file system management.
- Thirty percent of the questions relate to understanding DOS and Windows memory organization, managing memory conflicts, and optimizing memory usage on PCs.
- Thirty percent of the questions relate to installing, configuring, and upgrading operating system software on PCs, and cover boot sequences for each operating system mentioned.
- Twenty percent of the questions cover issues related to diagnosing or troubleshooting DOS, Windows 3.x, and Windows 95, including recognizing error messages during the boot sequence, operating system startup, and so on, and identifying steps to correct such problems. Also covered in this segment are printing issues, viruses, startup and INI files, and more.
- Ten percent of the questions deal with DOS and Windows networking topics, including sharing files and printers, working with network interfaces and protocols, and basic Internet access and service issues.

For more information about test topics and sample questions from each category of questions, please visit the DOS/Windows exam objectives page at **www.comptia.org/ct_aplus/html/body_dw_obj.html**. The exam code for the DOS/Windows exam is 220-102.

Network+

At this point, you'll take a detour from the normal structure of these chapters to learn a little bit about the vendor-neutral networking technician certification that CompTIA is currently creating. It's called Network+, and aims to define the same kind of basic competency and knowledge for network technicians that A+ presently defines for PC technicians.

CompTIA has had a task force working on the Network+ certification since 1995. Current participants include most major players in the computer networking industry, including Banyan, Compaq Computers, *ComputerWorld* magazine, DataTrain, Fluke, the Information Technology Training Association (ITTA), Lotus, Microsoft, the Network Professional Association (NPA), Novell, Softbank, U.S. Robotics, US West, Vanstar, and Wave Technologies.

Beyond its vendor neutrality, the Network+ certificate is supposed to recognize its holders' knowledge and understanding of networking tools, technologies, hardware, and software. Given the population of participating vendors and organizations, any testing regimen that this group can agree on should cover these bases quite well. Stay tuned to the Network+ home page at the CompTIA site for more information. You should expect to see announcements of the certification program's release and testing information by the end of 1998 or early in 1999.

A+ Testing

By now, you've read about both of the A+ tests, and are aware that similar tests may soon be available for the Network+ certification. You probably want to know what's involved in signing up for or taking such tests. Nothing could be easier than to explain!

To register for either or both of the A+ exams—and remember, you must take the second exam within 90 days of passing the first exam—call Sylvan Prometric at 800-776-4276 (or call 612-820-5200 outside North America).

To sign up for a test, you must have a valid credit card, or contact Sylvan for mailing instructions to send the company a check or money order. You will not be able to register for a test until payment has been verified or your check has cleared.

To schedule an exam, call at least one day in advance. To cancel or reschedule an exam, you must call at least one day before the scheduled test time (or you may be charged, even if you don't appear to take the test).

When you wish to schedule a test, have the following information ready:

- Your name, organization, and mailing address.
- Your Sylvan Test ID, which is an identifier that only you may use. (In the United States, this is your social security number. If you live outside the United States, call Sylvan to ask what kind of identification you need to provide when you take an A+ exam.) Outside North America, you may have to contact your local branch of the Association for Services Managers International (AFSMI) to arrange for A+ certification testing, if Sylvan does not operate a testing center in your area. For more information about this organization, please visit its Web site at **www.afsmi.org**, or contact AFSMI by phone at 941-275-7887.

- The name and number of the exam you want to take:
  - A+ Core exam: 220-101
  - A+ DOS/Windows exam: 220-102
- A method of payment.

Once you sign up for a test, you'll be told when and where the test is scheduled. Try to arrive at least 15 minutes early. You must supply two forms of identification, one of which must be a photo ID.

Both A+ exams are closed book. In fact, you can't take anything with you into the testing area; you will be furnished with a blank sheet of paper and a pen. I suggest that you immediately write down whatever you've memorized for the test before you start the test. You will have some time to compose yourself, to record this information, and even to take a sample orientation test before you begin the real thing. I suggest that you take the orientation exam; it will help you get more comfortable when you take the real test.

As soon as you complete your exam, the software tells you whether you've passed or failed. It also provides a report about your performance on various areas. Even if you fail the exam, I suggest you ask for—and keep—the test results that the test administrator can print for you. You can use these results to help you prepare to take the test again, if necessary. Alas, if you do need to take an exam again, you'll have to schedule another test, and pay the fee again.

How To Prepare For A+ Exams

At a minimum, you should use the following to prepare for the A+ tests:

- CompTIA provides pointers to plenty of training programs and study materials on its Web site, under the Training Materials button.
- Because CompTIA publishes test outlines and objectives for both the Core and DOS/Windows tests, it recommends that you familiarize yourself thoroughly with these items before taking any test. Test outlines are accessible through the two exam objectives Web pages mentioned earlier in this chapter.

In addition, you'll probably find any or all of the following materials useful in your search for A+ expertise:

- **Study guides** Numerous computer book publishers—including Certification Insider Press—offer A+ certification-related titles. I've picked over this crop, and found these titles to be informative and helpful for when you are preparing for the A+ tests, but that doesn't mean you shouldn't check the other publishers out too.

- **Other publications** You'll find plenty of other publications and resources if you take the time to look around on the Web or in your local bookstore, but there's no shortage of materials available about A+ test preparation.

This set of required and recommended materials represents a formidable collection of sources and resources for A+ exam topics and related information.

Need To Know More?

For convenience, I include the most important URLs mentioned so far in this chapter, along with pointers to a few other resources worth investigating for information about A+ certification, exams, training, and more.

www.comptia.org/ct_aplus/ This is the home page for A+ certification information, and includes access to guides about the A+ program, test objectives, test-taking information, and more. This should be your first stop in any search for A+ information.

www.amazon.com A quick visit to Amazon.com's search engine, using "A+ certification" as a search term, produced over a dozen titles, most aimed squarely at either the Core test or the DOS/Windows test. As long as you check to see which titles were published after May 1998 (when both tests were revised), these books will probably be quite helpful.

www.aplusexam.com The name of this site says it all—it's entirely devoted to helping its users take and pass the A+ exams. For $69, these folks will send you a CD-ROM that includes preparation materials, practice exams, and pointers to all kinds of useful stuff online.

www.gtspartner.com Global Training Solutions offers an A+ certification preparation program that's worth investigating. It offers 15 days' worth of training to help individuals prepare for both exams, plus a study kit that may be purchased separately.

www.mic-inc.com/aplus/ Marcraft also offers an A+ certification preparation program. It offers free practice tests as an enticement to visit its site; in addition, it provides a set of nearly 900 practice test questions for a relatively modest fee, and a certification study kit.

www.mindwork.com/aplusinfo.html Mindwork offers its own full-blown self-study materials and a quick prep guide for A+ certification for experienced PC technicians.

7

Sun's Java Certifications

Terms you'll need to understand:

- √ Java Development Kit (JDK) 1.0.2, 1.1, and 1.2
- √ Educational voucher ID

Techniques you'll need to master:

- √ Locating training and certification information on the Sun Education Web sites
- √ Deciding which of the Sun JDKs (1.02, 1.1, or 1.2) you wish to concentrate on
- √ Obtaining descriptions and objectives for the relevant Certified Java Programmer and/or Certified Java Developer exams
- √ Identify training and self-study options related to Java language certifications

Although Java is an extremely popular programming language, and is used in many large, successful companies—including Sun, Novell, IBM, and even Microsoft—Sun still controls licensing for this language. That's why Sun is also the source for Java certification credentials at present.

Right now, Sun offers two separate Java certification programs:

- **Certified Java Programmer** Candidates who seek this credential must have a strong working knowledge of Java language concepts, keywords, terms, and capabilities. Applicants must pass one exam that tests their knowledge of the Java language and its proper use and invocation. This represents the first rung in Sun's Java certification ladder.
- **Certified Java Developer** Candidates who seek this credential must first obtain the Certified Java Programmer credential for some valid JDK (currently, JDK 1.0.2 and 1.1 are valid, and have corresponding tests available; Sun is working to deliver tests for the 1.2 JDK by the end of 1998). The candidates must demonstrate their Java programming expertise by taking two tests: one to develop an application to Sun's specifications and the other to write an essay about the application they have written.

The ultimate source of information on Sun's Certified Java programs is the Sun Web site. The home page for certification information at Sun is **http://suned.sun.com/usa/cert_test.html**. From there, you can access just about anything related to this program, its tests, and other requirements, with the click of your mouse.

Java Certification Details

To begin with, let's review the two Certified Java programs that Sun has to offer. In that process, you'll have a chance to review the tests that you must pass to obtain each credential, including an overview, objectives, and so on. You'll also learn how to sign up for the tests, track progress toward either of Sun's Certified Java programs, and keep tabs on late-breaking Java certification news from Sun.

The first of the two programs is called the Certified Java Programmer program. Its goal is to verify an individual's basic knowledge of the Java programming language, in the context of some particular Java development environment, which Sun calls a Java Development Kit, or JDK. Currently, tests for two JDKs are available: Version 1.0.2—still in broad use and quite popular—is an early, stable release of the Java JDK; version 1.1—not as universally supported by Web browsers, especially older ones, but growing in popularity—is a later, more sophisticated release of the JDK.

To obtain credentials as a Certified Java Programmer, individuals must pass a single written exam. Each currently valid JDK has a separate test associated with it.

The second of the two programs is called the Certified Java Developer program. Its goal is to verify an individual's ability to develop Java-based applications and systems, again in the context of some particular JDK. Thus, versions of the tests are available for both the 1.0.2 JDK and the 1.1 JDK.

To obtain credentials as a Certified Java Developer, you must first obtain Certified Java Programmer credentials. Then, you must pass two additional tests: The first is called a performance-based test, and requires you to implement a Java application to meet a set of specifications furnished by Sun; the second is an essay based on your work for the performance-based test. Table 7.1 lists the criteria for each of the certifications.

> *Note: Sylvan handles only the Java Programmer test and the Java Developer essay tests; Sun Education handles the Java Developer performance tests (details are provided later in this chapter).*

In the sections that follow, you'll examine both of the Certified Java programs in more detail, and learn a little more about what's on the related exams. If you visit the URLs mentioned for each exam, in most cases, you'll be able to jump straight to the nitty-gritty details about each one.

STUDY ALERT

Although Web locations change over time, they're worth chasing down, because Sun's Web site is the best source for Java certification information and requirements. The home page for Sun certification information is **http://suned.sun.com/usa/cert_test.html**. From there, you can find all the details you might want quite easily.

Table 7.1 Java certifications: exams, questions, costs, time, and more.

Certification	JDK	Test ID	Questions	Cost	Time
Java Programmer	1.0.2	310-020	77	$150	135 min.
Java Programmer	1.1	310-022	60	$150	135 min.
Java Developer, performance test	1.0.2	N/A	N/A	$250	N/A
Java Developer, essay test	1.0.2	310-021	5-10	$150	90 min.
Java Developer, performance test	1.1	N/A	N/A	$250	N/A
Java Developer, essay test	1.1	310-024	5-10	$150	90 min.

Certified Java Programmer Program

As you've already learned, this program has but one exam that covers basic knowledge of Java language terms and keywords, concepts, and techniques. It aims to identify those individuals who understand the Java programming language and its proper use. The topics covered in this exam may be broken down as follows:

- Java language fundamentals, such as statement types and syntax, legal and illegal use of language constructs, and so on
- The use of operators and assignment statements in Java, including operator precedence, type handling, and so on
- Declarations and access controls in Java, such as variables, arrays, classes, member methods, default constructors, and calling methods
- Flow control and exception handling, including nested conditionals; conditional statements; use of **break** and **continue** keywords; flow of control constructs such as **try**, **catch()**, and **finally**; and use of exception-handling statements and techniques
- Overloading, overriding, runtime type, and object orientation handling when working with objects, classes, methods, and variables
- Garbage collection, including behavior of the Java Virtual Machine's garbage collection facilities, and points at which objects become eligible for collection as garbage
- Threads and thread-handling, including creating, using, and removing threads; state handling of threads; use of thread messaging tools and techniques; and so on
- Use of standard Java packages, including **java.lang**, **java.awt**, and **java.io**

For more information about this test, please visit the Java Programmer exam objectives pages located at **http://suned.sun.com/usa/cert_test.html**. From there, pick the Java Programmer JDK you wish to investigate, then click on the hyperlink labeled Exam Objectives. Likewise, click on the Sample Questions or Sample Questions With Answers hyperlinks to see practice questions (with or without the answers highlighted).

Certified Java Developer Program

For this certification, two tests are required beyond the Certified Java Programmer credential. The first is the unnumbered performance-based test, a programming assignment consisting of instructions and code that you must download from a special, password-controlled Web page on the Sun site. Then comes the numbered essay test. These two tests are distinct, and will exercise different aspects of your knowledge of Java programming.

The objectives for the programming assignment are as follows:

- Write an application program in Java, that incorporates these components:
  - A user interface that meets stated requirements for both static and dynamic elements.
  - A network connection that uses specified protocols to connect to an information server to obtain data for display within the user interface.
  - A multithreaded, threadsafe network server that connects to a specified Java database.
  - A database created by extending the functionality of supplied code for which limited documentation is available.
- Test the resulting application against a provided validation harness.
- List the significant design choices that were made during the implementation process, and discuss their advantages and disadvantages.
- Briefly justify choices that were implemented by comparing design and implementation objectives with their corresponding advantages and disadvantages.

Constructing the application requires knowledge of the following Java technologies and components: TCP/IP networking, I/O streams, GUI construction using standard AWT components, JDK 1.0.2 or 1.1 event model, object serialization, Javadoc, printing, packages, threads, and implementing interfaces.

The topics covered in the essay exam for the Certified Java Developer credential will vary, but normally demonstrate similar levels of coverage and interrelationships, as shown in the following list:

- Briefly describe, in four sentences or less, two approaches to inform the caller of a method that the called method has failed its operation. One of these approaches should be the one you implemented in your programming assignment.

- Briefly describe a total of no more than six advantages and disadvantages for each of the two approaches used to handle operations failures in a called method, in two sentences or less for each advantage or disadvantage.
- Briefly describe the approach you used in your assignment.
- Describe those specific design goals that informed your approach to the method you selected in your submission.

For more information about test topics and sample questions for this exam, please visit the Certified Java Developer exam objectives and sample questions pages at **http://suned.sun.com/usa/cert_test.html**. Remember to select the JDK that's appropriate for your chosen test.

Java Certification Testing

By now, you've read about the test for Java Programmer certification, and the two tests necessary for Java Developer certification. You probably want to know what's involved in signing up for or taking such tests. You can follow the same process for all the numbered Java certification tests—that is, for all tests other than the programming assignment for Java Developer, which you take through Sun Education. For information on the programming test, see the section later in this chapter titled "Registering For The Certified Java Developer Programming Assignment." But don't worry! If you get confused, you can always call a Sun Educational Services Representative for help at 800-422-8020 (outside North America, call 303-464-4097).

Registering For The Numbered Java Certification Exams

To register for any of the numbered Java certification exams, you must first call Sun Education to make arrangements for an educational voucher ID and to obtain the number for the nearest Sylvan Prometric center. Only then can you call Sylvan to arrange a date and time for your test.

> You can always call Sylvan at 800-755-EXAM, or 612-820-5200 outside North America, but you won't be able to sign up for a Sun test without first obtaining an educational voucher ID.

To sign up for a test with Sun, you have several choices. You can use a valid credit card, pay by purchase order if you have an established account with the company, or ask Sun Education for mailing instructions to send a check or money order. You can register for a test only after payment is verified or your check has cleared.

Once you have an educational voucher ID, you must then contact Sylvan to schedule an exam. Call at least one day in advance. To cancel or reschedule an exam, you must call at least one day before the scheduled test time (or you may be charged, even if you don't appear to take the test).

When you wish to schedule a test, please have the following information ready:

- Your name, organization, and mailing address.
- The Sun educational voucher ID.
- The name and number of the exam you wish to take.

Once you sign up for a test, you'll be informed as to when and where the test is scheduled. Try to arrive at least 15 minutes early. You must supply two forms of identification, one of which must be a photo ID. All Java certification exams are closed book. In fact, you can't take anything with you into the testing area; you will be furnished with a blank sheet of paper and a pen. I suggest that you immediately write down whatever you've memorized for the test before you start the test. You will have some time to compose yourself, to record this information, and even to take a sample orientation test before you begin the real thing. I suggest that you take the orientation exam; it'll help you get more comfortable when you take the real test.

As soon as you complete your exam, the software tells you whether you've passed or failed. It also provides a report about your performance on various areas. Even if you fail the exam, I suggest you ask for—and keep—the test results that the test administrator can print for you. You can use these results to help you prepare to take the test again, if necessary. Alas, if you do need to take an exam again, you'll have to schedule another test, and pay the fee again. Remember also that if you're pursuing Java Developer certification, after you complete the programming exercise part of the test through Sun Education, you must then contact Sylvan to schedule the essay part of the test with it.

Registering For The Certified Java Developer Programming Assignment

To sign up for this exam, you must first pass the Certified Java Programmer examination. Then, you must call Sun Educational Services at 800-422-8020 (outside North America, please call 303-464-4097) so that Sun can help you identify your local Sun Educational Services office. (You can also find a list of locations and phone numbers on the Web site, through the Java Certification home page on any of the Java Certified Developer Test Objectives pages.)

Next, you must call your local Sun Educational Services office and arrange for the $250 payment necessary to take this exam. Here again, a credit card will be your best option, but you can discuss alternative arrangements (including payment by purchase order, if you or your company already have an account open with Sun) with your local representative.

Once the payment has been received, you will be granted access to a special Web page where you can download the instructions and code for your programming assignment. You can take as long as you like to finish this assignment, but I recommend that you try to complete it within a month to keep yourself on track toward obtaining your certification.

How To Prepare For Java Certification Exams

At a minimum, you should obtain and study the following materials:

- Sun offers training courses and self-study materials to help you prepare for the various Java certification exams. Its JavaTutor on the Java Programming Library CD is a particularly worthwhile bit of self-study material (and may be ordered from Sun Education). For more information about courses and self-study materials, click on the Certification Courses or Self-Paced Products hyperlinks on the Java Certification home page at **http://suned.sun.com/usa/cert_progs.html**.
- Because Sun publishes test outlines and objectives for all its exams, it recommends that you familiarize yourself thoroughly with these items prior to taking any test. Test outlines are accessible through the Java Certification home page for all certifications and all current JDKs (except 1.2, which should appear by the end of 1998).

In addition, you'll probably find any or all of the following materials useful in your search for Java expertise:

- **Study guides** Most computer book publishers—including Certification Insider Press—offer Java certification-related titles or official documentation of the Java environment that are helpful for when you are preparing for the Java certification tests.

- **Other publications** You'll find plenty of other publications and resources if you take the time to look around on the Web or in your local bookstore, but there's no shortage of materials available about Java, if not directly on Java certification test preparation. A quick visit to Amazon.com turned up over 200 titles in its "Programming Languages-Java" category.

This set of materials represents a useful collection of sources and resources to help you prepare for Java certification exam topics and related information.

Need To Know More?

http://suned.sun.com/usa/cert_progs.html This is the home page for all Sun certification information, and includes ready access to information about the various Certified Java programs, including test objectives, sample questions, test-taking information, and much more.

www.amazon.com A quick visit to Amazon.com's search engine, using Programming Languages-Java as a search term, produced over 200 titles, many aimed squarely at either the certification tests or extremely relevant topics.

www.jars.com Jars is the Java archives online and a great source of information for just about anything Java-related. The Java Resources hyperlink on its home page points to tons of Web sites, newsgroups, and mailing lists that cover the Java world admirably, including certification.

There are numerous other members of the **comp.lang.java** Usenet newsgroup family. Here are some important ones:

- **comp.compilers.tools.javacc** Information about the standard Java compiler.
- **comp.lang.java.databases** Information about Java and databases.
- **comp.lang.java.gui** Information about Java-based user interfaces.
- **comp.lang.java.machine** Information about the Java Virtual Machine.
- **comp.lang.java.programmer** Programmer tools, tips, techniques, and more.
- **comp.lang.java.security** Discussion of security-related Java issues.

www.woj.com/tech/javacert/index.shtml This is the Web page for the Java Certification Exam Online Study group, maintained by Ian Wojtowicz.

http://forumsb.compuserve.com/gvforums/default.asp?SRV=JavaUser This is the Web page for the JavaUsers Forum on CompuServe.

Afterword

Although the formal portion of this book has concluded, I felt obliged to leave you with some additional bits of information. For one, I think it's important to acknowledge that the certification programs I've covered in this book don't begin to encompass the vast array of offerings or certifications that are available for people interested in technical computer certifications. That's why I include a section here called "Other Certifications," which mentions some more of the many certifications I didn't cover in this book.

Likewise, I include another section called "Making It All Make Sense," wherein I give you the chance to see how your interests, abilities, and experience stack up against the various certifications I've covered. For what it's worth, you can also use this same information to evaluate your potential relationship with other certifications, whether mentioned in this afterword or not.

Other Certifications

To start with, I'll mention a few additional certifications that you might find interesting, assuming that you found what I've already covered interesting as well. After that, I'll follow with a list of briefly annotated pointers to other certifications that you can chase down on your own, if what you see appeals to you.

One important ingredient in obtaining certification is training, whether it happens in the classroom or through self-study of some kind (using computer-based training, interactive Web sites, books, or whatever). Another important ingredient in getting people certified, therefore, lies in getting them trained. To that end, most vendors have additional certifications for trainers who are competent to teach such materials—for instance, Microsoft has a credential called the MCT, or Microsoft Certified Trainer, and Novell has a credential called the CNI, or Certified Novell Instructor. Likewise, most of the other vendors offer similar credentials for individuals who want to both learn and teach the subject matter that their certifications (and training programs) cover.

This leads us to what is—at least in my mind—the most important of the "other certifications" I'll cover here. I am referring to an organization known as the Chauncey Group (a subsidiary of the well-known company Educational Testing Services, the folks who offer the SAT and GRE tests to the world at large). The Chauncey Group offers a technical training certification known as the CTT, or Certified Technical Trainer. High-tech companies across the board, from Novell to Microsoft, accept possession of the CTT credential in lieu of their various "train the trainer" courses, which they otherwise require to obtain training credentials. Best of all, it only costs about $500 to become certified as a CTT, whereas completing the vendor "train the trainer" courses can easily cost $1,500 or more. For more information, visit the Chauncey Group's site at **www.chauncey.com/itt/cttp001.html**.

Bay Networks, one of the largest networking companies, offers a variety of certifications for users of its products, including specific credentials related to the company's hubs, routers, switches, and remote access and network management software products. For more information, visit its Technical Certification Study Guide home page at **http://support.baynetworks.com/training/study.html**.

The Network Professional Association (NPA) offers a core exam to certify network professionals. Like CompTIA's soon-to-be-available Network+ exam, this is a vendor-neutral exam that documents an individual's general knowledge of networking technologies, protocols, and practices. For more information, please visit the NPA Web site at **www.npa.org**.

Here's a brief list of URLs that provide information about other certifications that might be worth a look:

- **www.1stlookinc.com/certifi.html** This is the Web page of First Look Nationals, Inc. It mentions over 40 computer-oriented certification programs from a wide variety of vendors and organizations. Although it doesn't include pointers to these vendors' Web sites, it's a great place to see what's available.

- **www.compaq.com/training/aseinfo.html** Compaq offers a certification called the Accredited Systems Engineer, or ASE; visit the URL for more information. Be sure to check out its DEC- and Tandem-related certifications as well.

- **www.ibm.com/support/wwsup30e.nsf** IBM offers more than a dozen certification programs. It provides certifications on all of its major product lines as well as for each of its large subsidiaries (most notably Lotus Development Corp. and Tivoli Systems, Inc.). Visit this URL and then click on the Education & Certification hyperlink, to learn more about this company's wealth of certification offerings.
- **www.3com.com/support/mns/** 3Com, the networking products and services giant, offers a Master of Network Sciences certification, which you can read about here.

Making It All Make Sense

Given that I've covered certifications for everything from entry-level PC technicians (A+) to extremely senior internetworking experts (CCIE)—and many points in between—you might find yourself wondering: "How does all this apply to me?"

Unfortunately, there are no simple answers to this question, but you can figure out what's relevant to your interests and your career possibilities if you take the time to answer a few simple questions:

- **Does this certification match any of my prior knowledge or experience?** If the answer is yes, chances are good that you can jump into the related program with a minimum of difficulty, and without having to immerse yourself in the background knowledge necessary to master the subject matter. The better the fit between a certification and your prior experience and knowledge base, the easier that certification will be for you to obtain.
- **Does this certification seriously engage my interest or enthusiasm?** Without some motivation, going through the motions of obtaining a certification can be tedious and even overwhelming. Whether or not you already have the necessary background experience and knowledge, without interest and enthusiasm, you will have to work harder than you might like to obtain any certification you pursue.
- **Do the products, technologies, and knowledge related to this certification fit my current workplace? Do they fit my plans for a future workplace?** If the answers to both of these questions are "No," you'll probably want to pass on this one, unless you collect certifications the way others collect stamps or rocks. Because of the time and expense involved in obtaining certification—and the importance of hands-on experimentation and experience—chasing a certification on a topic when you don't have access to the software or hardware involved can be very frustrating.

- **Am I ready to spend evenings, weekends, and vacations chasing this credential?** Even entry-level certifications like the A+ take weeks, if not months, to prepare for and pass. Major certifications like the CCIE or MCSE+I can take more than a year to complete. This means spending all your spare time during that interval learning, studying, and practicing for the test(s), rather than watching a ball game or talking on the telephone. Are you really ready to make this sacrifice? If not, don't waste your money chasing something you won't finish.
- **By itself, is the certification enough to get me the job I want?** On the various certification-related mailing lists, we see young people asking if a certification is better than, or a reasonable substitute for, a college degree. The overwhelming response from people working in the field is "Stay in school!" Most large companies, and many small ones, won't even consider hiring someone as a technical employee without a college degree, no matter how many certifications the candidate has. Don't go thinking that certification is enough to get you into a high-paying job if you don't have some education and experience to go with it.
- **Can I afford to fail? Can I afford to pass?** Even your humble author has failed a couple of certification exams, and he writes books about this stuff. If you're financing your certification on a shoestring, what happens if the shoestring breaks? Clearly, chasing a CCIE when you don't have a couple of thousand dollars to spare for preparing could be a big mistake. If you have to retake a test that costs $1,000, can you really afford it? Even if you pass, can you really afford it? Be realistic about what you pursue—you can start out with an A+ for under $300, move up to an MCP for about the same amount, and then chase an MCSE for about $600, if you do things the inexpensive way. You might want to consider designing a ladder of certifications for yourself to climb, rung by rung, based on the complexity and expense of each rung. If you can land better-paying jobs at each step along the way, you can afford the increasing expense involved in climbing to the next rung.

Above all, you want to be comfortable chasing whatever certifications you pursue. If you're not the programmer type, don't even think about the Certified Java credentials. Likewise, if you don't aspire to run a large, complex network or work at a leading-edge ISP or communications company, a CCIE may not do you any good, even if you can get one. Try to fit your interests, your obsessions, and your strengths to these certifications and you'll succeed, no matter what you do.

So, let me wish you luck, and the joy of learning and experience, as you take the next steps down the road to the certification—or certifications—of your choice!

Glossary

A+—The name given to the exam created by the Computing Technology Industry Association (CompTIA) that is designed to certify individuals who are competent PC technicians, and whose knowledge covers hardware and software products, principles, and technologies from many vendors.

AATP (Authorized Academic Training Program)—A Microsoft term referring to an institution of higher learning (usually a community college, four-year college, or university) that offers the official Microsoft training curriculum under a special license to academic institutions.

adaptive tests—Tests that recognize when a test-taker misses a question, and pose simpler questions on the same topic, asking gradually more difficult questions on that topic until the test-taker's expertise (or lack thereof) in the category is established.

AFSMI (Association for Services Managers International)—A worldwide professional organization devoted to the areas of technical support and IT services management that cooperated with the Computing Technology Industry Association (CompTIA) to help develop its certification tests. For more information, visit its Web site at **www.afsmi.org**, or contact the company at 941-275-7887. Also known as AFSM International.

ATEC (Authorized Technical Education Center)—The location where you can take a Microsoft Official Curriculum course taught by Microsoft Certified Trainers.

CCDA (Cisco Certified Design Associate)—Cisco's entry-level design credential, which requires individuals to be able to design and deploy simple routed and switched networks, as well as configure, operate, and maintain them. To obtain this certification, applicants must pass a single exam.

CCDP (Cisco Certified Design Professional)—Cisco's middle-tier design credential, which requires individuals to be able to design and deploy complex routed LANs and WANs, plus switched LANs and LANE environments. Likewise, individuals must be able to configure, operate, and maintain such networks and connections. To obtain this certification, applicants must first obtain Cisco Certified Network Associate (CCNA) and Cisco Certified Design Associate (CCDA) certifications, and then pass either two or four exams, depending on which exam track they elect.

CCIE (Cisco Certified Internetwork Expert)—The top-tier operational Cisco certification, aimed at individuals who have advanced technical skills and knowledge, and who know how to configure networks for optimum performance. They must also understand how to maintain complex, far-flung, multivendor networks. Applicants must pass only two exams for this certification: a written exam and a laboratory evaluation.

CCNA (Cisco Certified Network Associate)—Cisco's entry-level operational certification, aimed at individuals who must manage simple routed LANs or WANs, small ISPs, or smaller switched LAN or LANE environments. Applicants must pass one exam to obtain this certification.

CCNP (Cisco Certified Network Professional)—Cisco's middle-tier operational certification, aimed at individuals who must install, configure, operate, and troubleshoot complex routed LANs, routed WANs, switched LAN networks, or Dial Access Services. Applicants must first obtain Cisco Certified Network Associate (CCNA) certification, and then take either two or four additional exams, depending on which test option they elect.

CDIA (Certified Document Imaging Architech)—A certification offered by the Computing Technology Industry Association (CompTIA), which also offers the A+ certification.

Certified Java Developer—A Java certification in which individuals must submit an application and pay a fee to receive a set of specifications for a full-blown Java application. They must then create an application to meet the specifications, and submit it to SunSoft for evaluation.

Certified Java Programmer—A Java certification in which individuals must take a written test aimed at a specific Java Development Kit (JDK).

CIP (Certified Internet Professional)—A Novell certification in which candidates prove their expertise on one or more of a variety of Internet professional roles: Certified Internet Business Strategist, Certified Web Designer, Certified Web Developer, Certified Intranet Manager, and Certified Internet Architect. To qualify, candidates must pass anywhere from one to five exams, depending on the role for which they seek certification.

Cisco—The market leader in routing and switching hardware. Cisco certification is among the most difficult of all vendor-based certifications.

CNA (Certified Novell Administrator)—Novell's entry-level certification. Obtaining a CNA requires passing any one of five tests: basic administration for three versions of NetWare (5, 4.11/IntranetWare, or 3.12) or for two versions of GroupWise (5 or 4).

CNE (Certified Novell Engineer)—The most sought-after Novell certification. CNEs specialize in a particular version of NetWare (presently 3.x, 4.x, or 5), and must pass five or six required tests (depending on the track) and one elective test to qualify.

CompTIA (Computing Technology Industry Association)—An organization that includes most major PC hardware and software manufacturers. This organization offers the A+ certification to provide vendor-neutral credentials for PC technicians who are ready and able to handle a broad variety of hardware, operating systems, and related matters. It also offers the CDIA (Certified Document Imaging Architech) certification.

DBA (database administrator)—A generic term for the job description of those individuals who must create and maintain databases.

ILT (Instructor-Led Training)—Oracle Education's comprehensive set of classroom courses for exam preparation and general training. Ultimately, the Oracle exams are derived from classroom experience with students, and Oracle indicates that ILT classes will always cover all the material necessary to take and pass the related test.

laboratory evaluation—The second test for the Cisco Certified Internetwork Expert (CCIE) certification. Applicants are subjected to a variety of simulated situations to test their hands-on abilities and diagnostic skills. They must implement a network or a communications environment from scratch, reconfigure existing environments, and troubleshoot multiple environments that have been deliberately misconnected, misconfigured, or otherwise messed with.

MBT (Media-Based Training)—Oracle's term for self-paced, computer-based training materials. There's a substantial overlap between MBTs available from Oracle and the various certification exams, but sometimes it's necessary to complete two MBTs to adequately prepare for an examination.

MCNE (Master CNE)—Novell's most elite certification, which designates recipients as certified specialists in one of seven areas of expertise. The requirements vary from specialty to specialty, but involve anywhere from four to six tests beyond CNE certification.

MCP (Microsoft Certified Professional)—A Microsoft certification that certifies anyone who's qualified for any Microsoft certification credential. It encompasses more than 60 exams at present. Passing almost any exam (except Networking Essentials, exam 70-058) qualifies an individual as an MCP. This is a stepping stone to the much-vaunted Microsoft Certified Systems Engineer (MCSE) credential, which requires passing six tests.

MCP+I (MCP + Internet)—A Microsoft certification that certifies Microsoft Certified Professionals (MCPs) who prove their Internet expertise, and who qualify to plan security, installation, and configuration of server products; implement server extensions; and manage server resources. Three core exams are required to pass.

MCP+SB (MCP + Site Building)—A Microsoft certification that certifies individuals who can design, build, and maintain corporate Web sites. It requires that individuals first become Microsoft Certified Professionals (MCPs), then pass any two from a pool of three tests.

MCSD (Microsoft Certified Solution Developer)—A Microsoft certification aimed at developers rather than systems or network managers. Candidates for this certification prove their abilities to build Web-based, distributed, or e-commerce applications. Knowledge of solution architectures, application development strategies and techniques, and development tools is required of all candidates, who must pass three core exams and one elective exam to qualify.

MCSE (Microsoft Certified Systems Engineer)—A Microsoft certification that certifies individuals who prove their expertise with desktop and server operating systems, networking components, and Microsoft BackOffice products. To qualify, candidates must pass six exams—four core exams and two electives.

MCSE+I (MCSE + Internet)—A Microsoft certification that certifies individuals who prove their expertise in using Microsoft products and technologies in Internet or intranet environments. Candidates must first become Microsoft Certified Systems Engineers (MCSEs), then pass three Internet core exams and two Internet-specific electives.

Microsoft—Currently the market leader in operating system technology and productivity applications. Microsoft offers the most varied selection of all vendor-based certifications.

Microsoft exam IDs—The numbers assigned to specific Microsoft certification tests. For example, the exam ID for the TCP/IP test is 70-059.

MOUS (Microsoft Office User Specialist)—The certification at the bottom of the Microsoft certification hierarchy. This program recognizes three levels of certification: a Proficient Specialist for Word and Excel, Expert Specialist for each of the Office components, and Microsoft Office Expert for those who are experts in all Office components and who pass an integration test to boot.

NetWare—A popular network operating system developed by Novell. The versions available are 3.x, 4.x, and 5.

network administrator—The individual responsible for the maintenance of a company's network.

Network+—A new exam (slated for delivery in spring 1999) from the Computing Technology Industry Association (CompTIA) that will aim to provide vendor-neutral credentials for network technicians (who seldom work in single-vendor environments, in any case).

Novell—The networking software giant that offers some of the most respected technical certifications available.

OCP (Oracle Certified Professional)—A catch-all term that identifies anyone who obtains an Oracle certification, either as a database administrator (DBA) or an Oracle application developer. DBA candidates must demonstrate their abilities to install, configure, manage, and maintain Oracle databases; software developer candidates must demonstrate their knowledge of Oracle design and development principles, plus important APIs, report generators, forms-based development tools, and so on.

Office User Specialist—*See* MOUS (Microsoft Office User Specialist).

OLA (Oracle Learning Architecture)—Oracle's term for its Web-based training materials. Although these are largely self-paced, and entirely computer-based, OLA training also includes the opportunity to interact with an instructor via email or online chat facilities. Thus, it strikes a balance between the ILT (Instructor-Led Training) and MBT (Media-Based Training) approaches.

Oracle—The leading relational database vendor in today's marketplace. Oracle's database products are used in many corporations and organizations around the world.

Oracle Certified Application Developer track—An Oracle certification that focuses on preparing database professionals to use Oracle's Developer/2000 Release 1 tools and technologies to build state-of-the-art, database-driven applications. It requires you to pass five tests.

Oracle7.3 Certified Database Administrator track—One of the tracks for Oracle Certified Professionals (OCPs). Obtaining this credential requires passing four tests.

program tests—Tests that use traditional, multiple-choice questions, graphical exhibits, and simulations. They follow a regular, predictable sequence of questions—drawn at random by category—from a database of potential questions. Everybody sees the same number of questions and gets an equal amount of time to finish.

system administrator—Generally, anyone who is responsible for managing and maintaining a computer system, usually a network server of some type. *See also* network administrator.

TechNet—A monthly CD subscription available from Microsoft.

Index

What's On The Companion Disk?

Take an interactive tour through the computer industry's most popular certification programs. Decide which one matches your professional goals and professional experience. Sample the types of questions found on the various exams and familiarize yourself with the Certification Insider Press learning approach—Learn It! Pass It! Do It! Learn with our *Exam Prep* Series. Get ready to pass the exam with the *Exam Cram* Series, the only books 100 percent focused on passing the exam. Use our *On Site* Series to make quick decision, troubleshoot, and save time and money on the job. Listen as our readers share their certification success stories.

- Meet Ed Tittel, the *Exam Cram* Series Editor and the author of this book
- Get all the facts on the hottest exams
- Learn why certification is your key to success in the computer industry
- Get a sneak preview of several popular exams

Software Requirements:

- Windows 95, Windows 98, or NT 4

Hardware Requirements:

Minimum:

- Pentium 100MHz
- 4X CD-ROM

We recommend:

- IBM Pentium 133MHz or above
- 6X CD-ROM or above